Glorious mothering

Sherry Hayes

Contents

Preface 1

Chapter 1
Moms Can Have Joy 7

Chapter 2
How to be a Self-controlled Mom 23

Chapter 3
How to Become a Peaceful Mom 31

Chapter 4
When You Should and Shouldn't Worry 37

Chapter 5
Overcoming Overwhelm 45

Chapter 6
Weathering a Storm 53

Chapter 7
Streamlining 65

Chapter 8
Getting Ahead 73

Chapter 9
Making Children Behave 81

Chapter 10
Keeping Track by Herding 95

Chapter 11
Harness the Potential Energy in Your Family for God's Glory 103

Chapter 12
Finding Time for Recharge. 109

Chapter 13
Troubleshooting 117

Chapter 14
Don't Make Your Kids Ashamed of Their Home 125

Homeschool Products by Sherry Hayes 132

Preface

As I am writing this my house is not in perfect order. Yesterday we had a carpet man come and steam clean our entire estate; all three floors, six bedrooms, three living areas, loft, and on and on...

In my garage is a mound of everything we took out in order for this gentleman to have access. There are boxes of books and their perspective shelves, knick-knacks, baskets, etc. On the front porch there are our under-the-desk plastic mat things (one was melted into a bowed shape by the sun--should be interesting trying to make it lie flat) all arranged in a helter-skelter manner and covered with muddy footprints.

The laundry is in flux; a few piles of dirty, a few piles of clean waiting to be folded.

There is a lot of work to be done this morning, but here I am, plugging away at my book, unworried, certain (actually in happy anticipation) that things will be put back in order in a few hours.

How can this be? How can a mom who is responsible for bringing 15 children into the world be calm and collected, even peaceful and unharried, in the midst of her life?

Part of It is Experience

Some young women know they are destined to be moms of many. I wasn't one of them. Children were oddities to me, and babies were a complete mystery. Neither my husband nor I were groomed to be successful at family life; divorce and brokenness have run like a huge, rotting crack down both sides of the family tree. Yet, here I am, happily married to my husband of 37 years with 36 of those filled with all of the joys and privileges parenting brings.

I'm now in my 50's, with four children in their 30's and the other 11 in various stages of growth and maturity. Some are learning how to parent their own children, others are learning to drive, some are simply learning who they are, still others are learning to read. I've known days when at least 10 children were sick with the stomach flu and I was the only one who could clean up and wash the sheets and blankets. I've had a toilet overflow until there were six inches of water all over the house when I was eight months pregnant. My children have rebelled, questioned their faith, or just decided they're too busy to give us a ring.

Many times I've seen the storms of life formulate, watched them rain in torrents, and then enjoyed cool refreshment as they dissipated. All of these experiences have done a great work; they have allowed me to see that God really and truly does work everything out according to His good purposes in us.

Yes, it's more than OK to have crazy days. Actually,

Glorious Mothering

it is quite normal and to be expected (the only people experiencing complete tranquility are the ones who are dead and buried).

Take it from me, a mom with 15 children who aren't naturally docile or compliant (actually, if I subscribed to the ABC-XYZ labeling scheme almost all of them would be on heavy medication. I mean it, I could tell you story after story!). Also, I am not naturally a high-energy person. I can become enthused and work in spurts, but I tend to like things slow and steady, something my children have never allowed me.

And yet, I am not a nervous wreck. I don't have patches of hair missing, and I don't go around with a constant frown muttering to myself in a gravelly voice.

If God can grace me to handle this surprising miracle every day, then He can grace you, too.

I am writing this book, not to condemn you, but to give you hope. I think you will sense the amount of prayer that has gone into its compilation (some chapters are based on posts from my blog, MomDelights.com, which were subsequently reworked and expanded, others are completely new). I have asked that God make each chapter encouraging and refreshing as you strive to build a home atmosphere filled with God's peace and glory.

It's God's enthusiasm that has seen me this far, and it will see you through, too. Here is a poem that always encourages me:

It Couldn't Be Done

by Edgar A. Guest

Somebody said that it couldn't be done
But he with a chuckle replied
That "maybe it couldn't," but he would be one
Who wouldn't say so till he'd tried.
So he buckled right in with the trace of a grin
On his face. If he worried he hid it.
He started to sing as he tackled the thing
That couldn't be done, and he did it!

Somebody scoffed: "Oh, you'll never do that;
At least no one ever has done it;"
But he took off his coat and he took off his hat
And the first thing we knew he'd begun it.
With a lift of his chin and a bit of a grin,
Without any doubting or quiddit,
He started to sing as he tackled the thing
That couldn't be done, and he did it.

There are thousands to tell you it cannot be done,
There are thousands to prophesy failure,
There are thousands to point out to you one by one,
The dangers that wait to assail you.
But just buckle in with a bit of a grin,
Just take off your coat and go to it;
Just start in to sing as you tackle the thing
That "cannot be done," and you'll do it.

Glorious Mothering

Glorious Mothering

Chapter 1

Moms Can Have Joy

Got grief? If you are a Christian mom, grief should be chasing you down daily. Why? Because there is a devil and he hates godly people. If the devil isn't coming against you it's because you're walking alongside him.

> Yea, and all that will live godly in Christ Jesus shall suffer persecution.
> 2 Timothy 3:12

> The wicked plotteth against the just, and gnasheth upon him with his teeth.
> Psalm 37:12

This is just what life on planet earth is about. We strive to receive the prize of knowing Christ, the devil tries to steal from us, kill us, and destroy us and everything we have and do.

But Wait, There's More...

The devil wants to make us think that we have no recourse, that we just have to cover our heads with our arms while the sky falls. He also leads us to believe that pain and suffering and depression are God's will for us in this life.

But He is a Liar

God does not want us sad and sorry and depressed. He wants us full of *joy* and *hope.*

When I first became a full-time mom I expected the worst. Everything I had read and witnessed taught me that women at home with children should become depressed and even looney. I believed the lie that if I didn't have anything outside the home to keep me busy I would automatically become a frumpy, ugly monster.

But that's not what God says. God has not only promised all of us joy, HE HAS SPECIFICALLY PROMISED *MOMS* JOY!

Yes, yes, yes it's true! Not only does God see moms at home who are pouring out their lives for their children, He has given them a specific promise they can rely on in every situation they face:

> He makes the barren woman abide in the house As a joyful mother of children. Praise the LORD!
> Psalm 113:9

Did you catch that? "As a JOYFUL mother of children," praise God!

And here is another secret that the devil is trying to keep from us: The kingdom of God is FULL of joy, and, for the believer, His kingdom is NOW.

8

You will show me the path of life;
In Your presence is fullness of joy;
At Your right hand are pleasures forevermore.
Psalm 16:11

If then you were raised with Christ, seek those things
which are above, where Christ is, sitting at the right
hand of God. Set your mind on things above, not
on things on the earth. For you died, and your life is
hidden with Christ in God.
Colossians 3:1-3

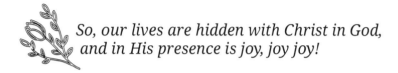

*So, our lives are hidden with Christ in God,
and in His presence is joy, joy joy!*

It doesn't seem logical, I know. We are accustomed
to trusting what we can touch, taste and feel, but there
is more to this life. The tangibles we experience every
day are not eternal, they are temporal. Now, everything
physical is not evil, but everything physical is subject to
the spiritual as we allow our minds to be renewed by the
Word of God so that our perspective is changed.

Here is a True-life Story...

We were in the midst of some enormous trials,
not ones that lasted a day or two, but the type that
lasted years. The struggle was tiring, exhausting even.
Somewhere in the mix was the idea that God wanted
us to suffer, so we should be good soldiers and trudge

along, carrying our hopelessness like a huge weight on our backs.

Then, one day, my son came up to me and asked me a question: "What do we pray for when we recite the Lord's Prayer?"

To which I answered:

> Thy kingdom come,
> Thy will be done,
> On earth as it is in heaven.

"And what exactly is happening in God's kingdom right now? Are they worried? Are they depressed? Are they carrying heavy weights of woe and discouragement?"

Finally, it dawned on me. It wasn't God who was bearing down on us, it was a lie of the enemy. Here is Psalm 16:11 again:

> You will show me the path of life;
> In Your presence is fullness of joy;
> At Your right hand are pleasures forevermore.
> Psalm 16:11

FULLNESS of joy

PLEASURES forever more

That's what God wants for us, *that's* the kind of God we serve.

Yes, in this world we will suffer tribulation, that was the realistic prediction Jesus left us with. We still may have babies who keep us up at night, the toilet may still clog, and the neighbors may think we're crazy, but God has promised we can live above and beyond all of these things. There is perfect peace promised to us if we keep our gaze on Him:

> You will keep him in perfect peace, whose mind is stayed on You, because he trusts in You.
> Isaiah 26:3

This isn't just a theory. It is real. I know because I have experienced it in the midst of attacks to every part of our lives (and, believe me, having 15 children means there are potentials of all sorts of trials and tribulations). The peace of God, the joy of God, is more tangible to me than any circumstance I face.

Swim Against the Current

I know that this is not a popular perspective. There are so many embittered souls who are willing to share one horror story after another, or who say, "Just wait until..."

It's easy to be a bright-eyed, first-time parent and confidently proclaim loudly that you will never be tired or cranky or discouraged. But when the children start coming, and the days are longer than your energy and there is more month than money, you begin to see things through different eyes.

This world is not a paradise, and children are not

angels. They are born lovely, with a natural connection with heaven. They are also born selfish, stubborn, smelly, and messy.

Without meaning to, we can become like accident statistics; just a pile of women who were defeated by the hardships of life. Or, we can become aware of the enemy's attempts to steal our joy and begin to fight to regain it!

Just as with everything else in life, we as mothers must make a choice: Will we allow the negatives of motherhood cloud our experience, or will we take parenting as an opportunity to grow in faith and grace and begin to "accentuate the positive" while attempting to remedy the negative?

Here are five ways the devil attempts to steal our joy, and ways we can fight him and win it back :

1. By Fear and Worry

Now, a parent who is not concerned about his/her children is not worthy to be called human! A certain amount of care and worry is not only warranted, but required. This is why I nag my children to brush their teeth and do their school work.

However, there is also a care that is based in fear which stems from a lack of understanding of who God is. If God is in heaven ready to bring the hammer down at any time, then we must cringe in fear and try and keep evil things from happening as much as possible.

Glorious Mothering

This type of fear and worry make the sweetest person crotchety and mean. Patience flies out the door and anger wells up into balls of fiery condemnation under such taskmasters.

How to Overcome: Through Faith!

If we serve the God of the Bible who tells us to rest securely in His secret hiding place, to believe that He cares for us more than He cares for sparrows or flowers, and Who has sent His Son to die (For God did not send His Son into the world to judge the world, but that the world might be saved through Him. John 3:17), then there is no reason for us to fret and fume over the trifles of life.

> It is vain for you to rise up early, to sit up late, to eat the bread of sorrows: for so he giveth his beloved sleep.
> Psalm 127:2

How to do this? By believing and actively rolling all of our care onto Him:

> Casting all your care upon him; for he careth for you.
> 1 Peter 5:7

This is something I practice on a regular basis. Whenever I feel some anxiety coming up over any issue, I visualize rolling the weight of it off of myself and onto God, and I feel the relief instantly.

2. By Comparison With Others

We can all fall into the trap of thinking that others have it easier or do things better or are more "normal" or holy than we are. This can cause us to put demands on our family members (even ourselves and God) for more finances, for different behaviors, for a different place to live, etc.

How to Overcome: By Contentment.

> But godliness with contentment is great gain.
> 1 Timothy 6:6

Life is not like a television show; there are no cookie-cut scripts.

For instance, our family does not live a 9-5, Monday through Friday schedule. Often we are having our family "down time" in the morning and homeschooling in the evening. For years we could only afford small rental houses that were not in the best parts of town (and at one time there were 11 of us in less than 1000 square feet!) Some of my children did not learn to read as soon as their peers, and so I had to learn to accept and love and understand them just as they were created, no matter how it made me look to prying relatives or the occasional snoopy neighbor.

It was important that I learned to thrive in each situation by seeing that God had made our family, our circumstances, and each person unique. Expecting our situation to line up with some perception of perfection was not only silly, it was destructive to my peace and the well-being of those I love.

> Jesus said to him, "If I want him to remain until I come, what is that to you? You follow Me!"
> John 21:22

3. Through Whining

No, not the plaintive complaints of small children, but the incessant murmurings of us, their mothers!

Of course mothering is hard work, but work is *wonderful!* Just ask any retiree who must sit for hours at a time with nothing to do. Being occupied with the care and nurture of young people is the most invigorating, meaningful vocation in all of the world. If you have the privilege of devoting your entire day to this marvelous task, don't spend the balance of your time complaining and moaning about your plight. This will only make you a royal pain and a drag to any conversation, not to mention what it will do to your own mental attitude and spiritual health.

> Do everything without grumbling or arguing,
> Philippians 2:14

How to Overcome: By Thankfulness and Positive Declarations.

> Give thanks in all circumstances; for this is God's will for you in Christ Jesus.
> 1 Thessalonians 5:18

> Rejoice in the Lord always: and again I say, Rejoice!
> Philippians 4:4

This takes a bit of overcoming the "flesh." It doesn't seem natural when you feel rotten or discouraged to belt out a "Thank You, Lord!" without sounding a bit sarcastic. But if you are miserable enough, or if your desire to please God is greater than your desire to live in the muck and mire of your own mind and emotions, then you will try it. Know this: Your spirit, the part of you that is eternal, is not tied to the emotions of your physical body.

> Therefore if any man be in Christ, he is a new creature: old things are passed away; behold, all things are become new.
> 2 Corinthians 5:17

> But I say, walk by the Spirit, and you will not carry out the desire of the flesh.
> Galatians 5:16

Here is a truth: What you speak with your mouth will affect how you think and believe. If you allow your tongue to run wild, it will fall into its natural groove of negativity. But if you begin to purposely harness your tongue, you can speak things your ears will hear that will do a job on your thinking, and then your emotions will follow suit!

If you persist in declaring thankful, positive things such as, "I love my job as mom! My children are such sweet treasures! I am so thankful for every situation today

Glorious Mothering

because I know God is working everything together for my good!" then you will eventually begin to feel thankful, joyful, and happy with your life!

Don't believe me? Try it just for one week and see-- what can you lose except for a bit of misery?

4. By an Overcomplicated Life

There are so many choices, but so little time! This is the bane of our modern existence, isn't it? With the advent of the Internet, even someone buried under the snow in Alaska has a million things to participate in each day, with real people in "real time."

If we aren't being immersed in chat after chat, then there is always the temptation to have a "Pinterest" life...you know, the perfect specialty dinners served on bone China with monogrammed napkins and cupcakes decorated with garnished frosting. Or perhaps perfectly designed homes with all of the touches that show we care about artful living. It's sort of the Martha Stewart syndrome all done up with links and graphics.

Then there are the demands of community. One or two church services a week are never enough; there are Bible studies and prayer meetings and then the fund-raisers, not to mention soccer and softball practice, a community garage sale, and on and on and on...

(Remember Mary and Martha.)

Now, all of these things can be wonderful and can give

us abundance of relationships and memories, but only if done in *moderation*. Living on the fly, rarely allowing our feet to touch the runway, will keep us from the most important things. It will drain our energy, our health and our piggy banks and eventually tear down the intimacy of our families.

> All things are lawful, but not all things are profitable. All things are lawful, but not all things edify.
> 1 Corinthians 10:23

How to Overcome: By Simplifying and Focusing on What is Most Important

If you must chat and spend time online, make it a "reward" for when you have caught up on your housework and your "in real life" relationships. Use a timer and allow yourself 15 minutes to keep from going off on wild rabbit trails that keep you from paying attention to the most important things, such as kissing boo-boos, reading stories, cooking dinner, and folding laundry.

Also, trying to make everything "special" and perfect will only make everything seem boring and overdone. This means things like having simple meals that are filling and delicious as everyday fair mixed with exceptional meals or other treats reserved for special occasions. Then your life will become easier and you won't be rearing children who are so glutted they can't enjoy or appreciate anything.

18

Next, take a look at all of the activities you participate in. Pair them down to one or two that really add value to you and your family, and politely bow out of all of the others. Instead of being stretched so thin you are no good to anyone, you will find that the people and groups you *do* focus on will appreciate you more! (in some seasons of life this may mean that we are simply mommies at home--treasure these times, for they are fleeting!)

5. By Guilt

If there was ever a sure-fire bait enticing women to put the hook into their mouths, it would have to be angst and guilt.

Oh, how we love to do post-mortems on every word and action. We waste so much time going over what we have said or done that we rarely have time to think of how we can overcome. We don't allow our minds to rest so God can speak to us!

Here is a truth: Going over and over what we may have done wrong is not about repentance, it is about self-centered pride. No, none of us was ever perfect except for Jesus, and even He said that only God was good!

> For in many things we offend all. If any man offend not in word, the same is a perfect man, and able also to bridle the whole body.
> James 3:2

How to Overcome: Remember This Very, Very

Essential Truth:

> Above all, keep fervent in your love for one another, because love covers a multitude of sins.
> 1 Peter 4:8

As your love covers those who sin against you, God's love covers you.

If you make a mistake, ask God's forgiveness, then apologize for it, try to make it right, and get over it and get on with your life!

> Brethren, I count not myself to have apprehended: but this one thing I do, forgetting those things which are behind, and reaching forth unto those things which are before, I press toward the mark for the prize of the high calling of God in Christ Jesus.
> Philippians 4:13-14

The devil wants to keep you in bondage to your sins and mistakes, but God wants to see you set free so that you can go on to fulfill His will for you in Christ!

> It was for freedom that Christ set us free; therefore keep standing firm and do not be subject again to a yoke of slavery.
> Galatians 5:1

> For by grace you have been saved through faith; and that not of yourselves, it is the gift of God; not as a result of works, so that no one may boast. For we are

20

> His workmanship, created in Christ Jesus for good
> works, which God prepared beforehand so that we
> would walk in them.
> Ephesians 2:8-10

This includes those times when you lose your temper, spend too much time on the phone or computer, put off doing the dishes, etc.

How marvelous to realize that God has sent us the Holy Spirit to help us obey Him!

> I will ask the Father, and He will give you another
> Helper, that He may be with you forever; that is
> the Spirit of truth, whom the world cannot receive,
> because it does not see Him or know Him, but you
> know Him because He abides with you and will be in
> you.
> John 14: 16-17

Yes, it is possible to be a busy, hard-working mama and still have joy in abundance. Did you know that your joy and enthusiasm can overtake your whole body and rid you of many of your aches and pains while restoring your energy? Just think of the mom you can be to your children, not to mention the wife you can be to your husband.

The devil wants to keep us in bondage, but Christ wants to set us free–praise His name!

> If the Son therefore shall make you free, ye shall be free indeed.
> John 8:36

Chapter 2

How to Be a Self-Controlled Mom

There is a wild gal within me, and she is SO MUCH FUN!

She whoops and hollers at football games. She waves and dances in church.

She plays worship music really, really loudly and mouths the words while she vacuums. She buys chocolate for the kids and then eats it all on the way home.

Spontaneity is her best bud. She can wheel around on a dime or change course and charge ahead in a completely different direction.

And the Projects...

She can think of something new and creative almost every minute of every day. Pinterest is like candy, and she can gorge herself until she is about to burst with enthusiasm.

She loves passionately, laughs hilariously, fights valiantly.

But Sometimes...

She leaves a wake of destruction as she passes.

She says things without thinking or shares too much, whoops at the wrong time, stands up and dances when everyone else is sitting down.

When the projects become "work," or when she becomes bored and loses interest, they are stacked up in the corner, never to be finished. As soon as a creative, new routine becomes "routine" she tosses it in the trash.

Her passion can turn to disgust, her laugh into a pouting pity-party, her fight for all the wrong things.

In actuality, listening to the Wild Gal throws my life into turmoil, and turmoil makes me sick.

There is only one way to tame her:

SELF-DISCIPLINE: The ability to control one's feelings and overcome one's weaknesses; the ability to pursue what one thinks is right despite temptations to abandon it.

Yes, those words, the ones that conjure up shackles and prison matrons in starched gray uniforms with scowls on their faces are just what I need in my life.

In fact, all moms need self-discipline because all moms need FREEDOM!

I know what you are thinking, "Sherry, there is no way self-discipline will make me free. What I need is less responsibility, more money, kids that help out, a husband that understands, and a robot that does dishes!"

Really? I don't think so. I believe people who have less

responsibility, more money, and maids to do everything for them are some of the most imprisoned people on the earth. No amount of money or absence of demands can help someone who can't control themselves. If you really sit down and think about it, lack of restraint leads to chaos, and chaos is the defining characteristic of hell.

Venting, Expressing, and Indulging Lead to Slavery

> Like a city whose walls are broken through is a person who lacks self-control.
> Proverbs 25:28

Unfortunately, that's where we live some days, in our own hell on earth. We live in chaos because we are unable to control our emotional ups-and-downs. We fly from one thing to another, from one "mood" to another, because we have no anchor, no hope, no strength.

> So I find this law at work: Although I want to do good, evil is right there with me. For in my inner being I delight in God's law; but I see another law at work in me, waging war against the law of my mind and making me a prisoner of the law of sin at work within me. What a wretched man I am! Who will rescue me from this body that is subject to death? Thanks be to God, who delivers me through Jesus Christ our Lord!

> So then, I myself in my mind am a slave to God's law, but in my sinful nature a slave to the law of sin.
> Romans 7:21-25

When I was born again, there was a definite change in my life. Immediately there was a strength that emanated from somewhere deep inside me, one that helped me to overcome my own passions. I didn't understand it at the time, but it was unmistakable. If you are twice-born, you know what I am talking about. It was as if I was a totally new person, and I *was*.

> Therefore if any man be in Christ, he is a new creature: old things are passed away; behold, all things are become new.
> 2 Corinthians 5:17

And with this new creation, we are given a new Spirit:

> For the Spirit God gave us does not make us timid, but gives us power, love and self-discipline.
> 2 Timothy 1:7

This is the place of freedom in Christ. We are no longer bound by a set of unattainable standards and rigid rules. But this is where we often misunderstand; the rules have not been done away with, they have become part of our make-up. We don't wear them on the outside, they are part of every cell, down to our DNA.

> This is the covenant I will make with the people of Israel after that time," declares the LORD. "I will put my law in their minds and write it on their hearts. I will be their God, and they will be my people.
> Jeremiah 31:33

> Those who live according to the flesh have their minds set on what the flesh desires; but those who live in accordance with the Spirit have their minds set on what the Spirit desires. The mind governed by the flesh is death, but the mind governed by the Spirit is life and peace.
> Romans 8:5-6

Did you read that? LIFE and PEACE. That's what it means to have the Spirit operating in our lives, the reason we seek to overcome ourselves. Our rewards are the abundant life Christ promised and the peace that passes all understanding.

After all, it's not about our physical surroundings, it's our reactions to them. It's whether or not we listen to the emotions conjured up by a flesh that is set on immediate gratification. It's about allowing the Spirit within to cancel out the voices in our minds.

> Don't you know that when you offer yourselves to someone as obedient slaves, you are slaves of the one you obey--whether you are slaves to sin, which leads to death, or to obedience, which leads to righteousness?
> Romans 6:16

We Are Not Free To Disobey, We Are Free To Obey, Willingly, With Joy

Finally, we can have victory over destructive habits and

tendencies that stand in the way of true freedom. We can overcome our*selves*.

> He who is slow to anger is better than the mighty,
> And he who rules his spirit, than he who captures a
> city. Proverbs 16:32

> But the fruit of the Spirit is love, joy, peace, patience,
> kindness, goodness, faithfulness, gentleness, and
> self-control. Against such things there is no Law.
> Galatians 5: 22-23

We get there by following Paul's advice in Romans 12:2:

> Do not conform to the pattern of this world, but be
> transformed by the renewing of your mind. Then you
> will be able to test and approve what God's will is—
> his good, pleasing and perfect will.

And again he goes into greater depth in Ephesians 4:17-24:

> So I tell you this, and insist on it in the Lord, that
> you must no longer live as the Gentiles do, in the
> futility of their thinking. They are darkened in their
> understanding and separated from the life of God
> because of the ignorance that is in them due to the
> hardening of their hearts. Having lost all sensitivity,
> they have given themselves over to sensuality so as
> to indulge in every kind of impurity, and they are full
> of greed.

That, however, is not the way of life you learned when you heard about Christ and were taught in him in accordance with the truth that is in Jesus. You were taught, with regard to your former way of life, to put off your old self, which is being corrupted by its deceitful desires; to be made new in the attitude of your minds; and to put on the new self, created to be like God in true righteousness and holiness.

That's what it all boils down to, what we need to remember over and over. Our spirits are new, but our minds are *not*.

Notice here that Paul makes it clear; the transformation of our flesh is not automatic, it takes effort. Our minds need to be changed, transformed, and there is only one way to do it; by meditating on the Word of God.

For the word of God is alive and active. Sharper than any double-edged sword, it penetrates even to dividing soul and spirit, joints and marrow; it judges the thoughts and attitudes of the heart.
Hebrews 4:12

This Book of the Law shall not depart from your mouth, but you shall meditate in it day and night, that you may observe to do according to all that is written in it. For then you will make your way prosperous, and then you will have good success.
Joshua 1:8

Instead Of Giving In To The Wild Gal, I Have Wrestled Her Down And Changed Her Way Of Thinking

By constant meditation in the Word of God, I have pointed her in a fresh direction.

Her ears are tuned in to a different station. She takes her passionate energy and uses it for God's glory.

She doesn't call attention to herself. She points to Jesus.

She isn't afraid of work or tedium; walking with God makes every task worthwhile because her focus is on the eternal.

Before she starts a project, she prays and listens for the voice of the Holy Spirit. He leads and guides her so that her energy, time, and money are not wasted.

She still loves, laughs, and fights, but for all the right reasons, at the right times.

Do You Have A Wild Gal On The Inside, Too?

Chapter 3

How to Become a Peaceful Mom

Moms can, and must, find peace. When they don't, they become a menace to their families.

I know all about it, *peace* that is, and that's saying a lot. People don't believe me. They say it's not possible for a mom of 15 to know even the meaning of the word, but I do. I may even have more insights into the subject than the "experts."

I actually googled, "How to find peace" just to see what the general consensus on the subject might be. Can I say that the methods suggested were definitely not written with mothers in mind? Let me share just a few of the highlights:

"Go to a café and sip coffee slowly while you watch people sit and read the newspaper."

I can just imagine this one! While I'm sitting sipping coffee slowly, the children are fighting over the sugar container. The other patrons aren't reading their newspapers (and they are no longer sitting in the café) because of all of the chatter and noise we are creating.

"Get a good night's sleep."

Ha! I gave that one up about 15 babies ago. I'm so used to interrupted sleep that it is my normal, even though we don't have infants in the house anymore. By necessity I have learned to fall asleep instantly after any interruption and take advantage of every opportunity, even if this means catching a quick nap sitting in a chair or even standing up.

"Visit a garden in Paris."

This one has to make you want to roll on the floor holding your sides. I'm not kidding, it was actually on someone's list! I could imagine a mom saying, "I need some peace and tranquility. Pack up kids, we're off to Paris to visit a garden!"

"Fill your home with rocks, flowers, and candles."

Well, we often have rocks in the house, and I have been presented with quite a number of wilted wildflower bouquets. But when we talk candles we are thinking flames and screams and fire extinguishers...

I'm Sure Your Experiences Are Similar!

In order to create the perfect, tranquil environment I would have to nag my husband to death and lock my children in a closet. Since neither idea is acceptable to me, I have had to look at the subject from a different angle.

In the early years I would bounce back-and-forth

and up-and-down according to environment and circumstances. Then I discovered a something awesome:

Your environment does not create your peace; your peace creates your environment.

So, the trick is not to create the perfect home (decor, children, husband, etc.), but to become so peaceful that it flows out into all the other parts of your life. This happens because:

A Peaceful Mom Can Think More Clearly

She isn't flustered by crying babies or childish noise. She can do more than put two thoughts together, she can manage multiple tasks and projects in multiple parts of her life all at the same time.

Her thoughts are aligned and in order because they are not disturbed by conflict and unrest.

A Peaceful Mom Can Plan More Carefully

The tranquility of her thought patterns enable her to look into the future with positive creativity. As the Bible says, "she can laugh at the days to come" (Proverbs 31:25).

A Peaceful Mom Can Face Crisis and React Correctly

She isn't disturbed by spilled milk. When the washing machine breaks down she doesn't lose focus. She doesn't take her frustrations out on her husband or her children.

She can come up with positive ways to face and overcome obstacles instead of buckling under them and giving in to despair.

All great benefits, right? I don't think there is one mom reading this who isn't craving this kind of life. I'm telling you right now that any mom can have all this and more, if she realizes this great rule:

The true path to peace is not paved with effort. It is paved with abandonment.

Peace, the type that brings all the benefits mentioned above, doesn't rest on feelings, it rests on solid facts. Here are the facts that make the foundations of my peace as firm as bedrock:

God is a Good God and His Plans for Me Are Good

> For I know the plans I have for you," declares the LORD, "plans to prosper you and not to harm you, plans to give you hope and a future.
> Jeremiah 29:11

I am on His side, and He is on my side. He gives me everything I need, "I shall not want." Jesus prayed that God's kingdom would come to earth, a kingdom filled with love, joy, and light!

Glorious Mothering

In Every Circumstance God is Working for My Good

> And we know that in all things God works for the
> good of those who love him, who have been called
> according to his purpose.
> Romans 8:28

This includes teen meltdowns, financial challenges, feelings of isolation, attacks from the outside. There is always a kernel of His goodness, a problem that in its solving can only become a blessing.

If I keep my gaze on Jesus, I can enjoy the benefits of heaven no matter what my circumstances might be.

There is no way to describe how much this blesses me! There have been times when everything was turned upside-down and I was forced into situations where nothing was familiar. But Jesus was always there, His presence sweeter than ever.

This is something the world cannot experience or understand.

I recall a story about a dear believer suffering under a tyrannical regime for her faith. Her captors were frustrated because every time they tortured her her face would light up in a huge smile. When they asked her why, she told them that when they were beating her she would close her eyes and see Jesus standing with her and His presence filled her with peace and joy. Their solution? To tape her eyes open. Did it work? Of course not--her vision of Jesus continued no matter what they tried.

How can evil fight against something like that? It can't!

> Thou wilt shew me the path of life: in thy presence is fullness of joy; at thy right hand there are pleasures for evermore.
> Psalm 16:11

With all these things in mind, I can't help but release my worrying, fretting, and negative reacting. NO MATTER WHAT HAPPENS I can rest peacefully knowing that God is big enough to take care of it.

We don't have to carry it, all of the diapers, the laundry, the bill paying, the homeschooling. We can release it into the huge hands of our majestic, marvelous, magnificent Heavenly Father.

> Casting the whole of your care [all your anxieties, all your worries, all your concerns, once and for all] on Him, for He cares for you affectionately and cares about you watchfully.
> 1 Peter 5:7 (Amplified version)

Hallelujah! I just have to finish this chapter quickly so I can go dance and sing...I have written myself happy!

> Be anxious for nothing, but in everything by prayer and supplication with thanksgiving let your requests be made known to God.
> Philippians 4:6

Chapter 4

When You Should and Shouldn't Worry

Sometimes we misunderstand just what Jesus meant when He said we must be "careful for nothing."

It takes a care-full person to raise a family well, to be a good employee, to be responsible with money, and keep up a house. These are necessary concerns, and they are actually beneficial, not only to others, but to ourselves.

The Holy Spirit has gone to great lengths to warn us against a life that tends to throw off all concern for earthly things. Proverbs is rife with passages dealing with the slothful.

> The soul of a lazy man desires, and has nothing; But the soul of the diligent shall be made rich.
> Proverbs 13:4

> The way of the lazy man is like a hedge of thorns, But the way of the upright is a highway.
> Proverbs 15:19

Even in the New Testament we are told to work "while

it is still day," and Paul the Apostle discusses his concerns for the different flocks that were scattered all over the known world.

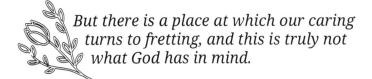

But there is a place at which our caring turns to fretting, and this is truly not what God has in mind.

We Need to Repent

Make no mistake, worry is *sin*. It accuses God of either not being *capable* of caring for us or not being *willing* to care for us. It is as if we are calling Him a liar and a hypocrite; as if while telling *us* to take care *He* is sitting back dozing in negligent ambivalence.

Besides this, fretting is not a harmless way of dealing with stress. I know this because I come from a long line of champion worriers (this activity is so popular on my side of the family it is practically an Olympic sport. The women, especially, compete for metals for exhibiting the most anxiety over a person or situation). Growing up I was taught that peace and confidence in God's loving care are sins more serious than murder.

The consequences of such thinking are not pretty.

Worry is all about fear, and fear leads to all sorts of other nasty sins. Anger is one of the worst. People who are anxious are irritable, touchy, unpredictable and prone to emotional outbursts.

38

They forget things easily because their minds are so cluttered. Whatever good they try to do is always tainted by their need to control everyone and everything so that nothing bad will happen.

Manipulating, slandering, lying, cheating, and stealing are all wrapped into the awful package when worry takes over a life.

Salvation and Renewal

As a large family mom, I have more to be care-full about than most people will ever understand. However, even after having 15 children, I am not fearful and angry. I am able to be joyful, smiling, enjoying life with my family and being creative in every area.

Even so, I am still tempted from time-to-time to fall back into a pattern of thinking that is so familiar and ingrained in my mind. This is why I am filled with compassion for those who struggle constantly and greatly desire to be free.

And you *can* be free. If you are born again, within you is a person who is filled with faith (2 Corinthians 5:17), one that lives in love, joy, peace, kindness and all the other fruits of the Spirit (Galatians 5:22-23).

Remember, He has not given us the spirit of fear, but of power, love, and self-control (2 Timothy 1:7).

As I have turned my mind from my own creature-thoughts, as A. W. Tozer calls them, to God's thoughts, my entire life has been changed according to Romans 12: 1-2.

He Has Solutions for Us

God is not a masochist. He would not have ordered us to stop fretting and then left us without the means to obey. He has actually buried the keys to living care-free lives in His Word. In the beginning of my mom life, when I had seven children under the age of 10 (and I was only 29), God showed me some of his keys while reading through Charles Spurgeon's commentary on Psalm 37. The very first verse tells us to "Fret not," and then we are told what to do instead starting in verse three:

Trust in the LORD

Spurgeon says:

Faith cures fretting. Sight is cross-eyed, and views things only as they seem, hence her envy: faith has clearer optics to behold things as they really are, hence her peace.

We trust in God because He is trust*worthy*. He created the heavens and the earth, He sent His only Son to die for us, He has sealed us with His Holy Spirit, and His goodness is spoken to us every morning in the rising of the sun. Certainly He is more sure than any other person or institution we may have trusted here on earth!

Do Good

Spurgeon says:

Glorious Mothering

True faith is actively obedient. Doing good is a fine remedy for fretting. There is a joy in holy activity which drives away the rust of discontent.

It's amazing how difficult it is to worry when we decide to do something positive and constructive. I've developed the habit over the years to find a cleaning or organizing project when I am awaiting some news or when things are unsure in my life. It is also very helpful to think of someone in need and offer a helping hand or even to send off a sweet note of encouragement. I often find that reading aloud a good book to my tiny ones or even switching the laundry will help keep me from nervous anxiety.

Delight Yourself in the LORD

Spurgeon says:

Make Jehovah the joy and rejoicing of thy spirit. Bad men delight in carnal objects; do not envy them if they are allowed to take their fill in such vain idols; look thou to thy better delight, and fill thyself to the full with thy more sublime portion. In a certain sense imitate the wicked; they delight in their portion -- take care to delight in yours, and so far from envying you will pity them. There is no room for fretting if we remember that God is ours, but there is every incentive to sacred enjoyment of the most elevated and ecstatic kind. Every name, attribute, word, or deed of Jehovah, should be delightful to us, and in meditating thereon our soul should be as glad as is the epicure who feeds delicately with a profound relish for his dainties.

This is the funnest part! If it weren't for Spurgeon's explanation of this verse I would have missed out on the finest joys I have experienced on earth. Relish in God, sing about His magnificence, speak of His glory, put all of your emotions into praise.

Commit Your Way to the LORD

Spurgeon says:

Roll the whole burden of life upon the Lord. Leave with Jehovah not thy present fretfulness merely, but all thy cares; in fact, submit the whole tenor of thy way to him. Cast away anxiety, resign thy will, submit thy judgment, leave all with the God of all.

This is a crucial step. When we have done all, we rest all things in His hands. I sometimes find myself physically casting my hands to heaven, as if I am casting my cares upon Him. I have even been known to write a concern, or list of concerns, on a piece of paper and then either tearing the paper up or burning it as a physical sign of the intangible faith on which I stand.

Proverbs 3:5-6 promises that when we commit our way to the Lord, He puts it all to rights, or "He will make your paths straight."

Also, Philippians 4:6-7 tells us that when we let God in on our troubles with thankfulness, He will cover our hearts and minds with a peace that goes beyond our ability to understand. How precious when we have a sense of peace that transcends even our feelings, a

Glorious Mothering

knowing that our future is sure in God's hands, no matter how things may look in the present.

> Be careful for nothing; but in every thing by prayer and supplication with thanksgiving let your requests be made known unto God. And the peace of God, which passeth all understanding, shall keep your hearts and minds through Christ Jesus.
> Philippians 4:6-7

Take Advantage of Good Training

It has been said that having a large brood of children can force you into a fretful, fearful existence, but I have found just the opposite to be true.

As I have weathered one storm after another over the years, God has created a scrap book of memories for me by gathering together snapshots of His faithfulness.

The times I thought were going to be the worst turned out to be the best. Times when misfortune threatened to dominate our lives we were pleasantly surprised by blessing after blessing, even if we still had to endure hardship or pain.

I probably have more to worry about today than when I first began having children, but I actually worry *less*, because *I trust more*.

And I think this is the purpose of the whole exercise; to learn to hold on to less and to let go of more until we are completely swallowed up in every facet and nuance of who He is, instead of being dominated by the physical world in which we live.

Chapter 5

Overcoming Overwhelm

There are times when we feel like our life is a jumbled box of puzzle pieces. We know the end result is a picture of a restful ocean scene, but we are so overwhelmed by the chaotic mess before us we don't know where to start.

Whenever I am feeling overwhelmed it is usually because of my own thinking, not circumstances. So, I stop everything and sit and think about where I got off track.

Here are some of the questions I ask myself:

Is My Mind Cluttered With Worry?

As we discussed in the last chapter, this is very important. When we are worried, we are prone to confusion and fretting, which leads to anger and destructive behavior.

If we don't know the Savior, we have every reason to be fretful, because we don't have a God who is near and dear and able to overcome every obstacle in and through us. If we *do* know the Savior and we are still worrying, we need to get back onto the side of faith, believing that God is working each and every circumstance for our good according to Romans 8:28.

> And we know that all things work together for good to them that love God, to them who are the called according to his purpose.
> Romans 8:28

Remember, *faith pleases God!*

> But without faith it is impossible to please him: for he that cometh to God must believe that he is, and that he is a rewarder of them that diligently seek him.
> Hebrews 11:6

Every mother of many children experiences numerous trials, ranging from paying the bills to having clean underwear, but only the foolish ones try and carry the whole load. Prudent mega-moms learn early-on to cast their cares on the Lord!

Otherwise, you will run around in circles "like a chicken with her head cut off," and will eventually run out of steam and give in to chaos.

When my own children were tiny and unable to help there were very few I could reach out to. I didn't dare call on relatives for fear of dealing with questions such as, "Why did you have so many children if you can't handle them?"

But I always had Jesus, and learning to roll everything onto His broad shoulders made my load lighter and my life brighter. Subsequently, many have marveled at how joy-filled I am! My mind is clear to work on tomorrow because I don't fear it. I look forward to the blessings God will bring to me, even through the trials!

> Casting all your care upon him; for he careth for you.
> 1 Peter 5:7

Am I Inventing Distractions to Keep Me From Taking Care of Unpleasant Tasks?

This is not just a question for mothers of many, it is something top-ranking businessmen ask themselves regularly.

It is human nature; we run *towards* things that are fun or feed us, we run *from* those things that are simply no fun at all, such as cleaning out the freezer or going through old bills (it is amazing just how many ways I can keep myself busy so that I don't have time to look at that ominous stack of papers to file in the office).

One dear woman decided that housework caused her stress and depression, but shopping filled her with energy. So, whenever it was time to do a sink of dishes or wash some clothing, she would hit the mall instead! She would feel so good at the store; everything was so neat, the people were all so friendly, and she enjoyed finding "bargains."

When she returned home with her purchases she was faced with the same filthy kitchen and pile of dirty clothing, so she would throw her bags somewhere in the corner and go out for dinner! This continued until her home was unlivable, her daughter was taken away, and her husband divorced her.

She is not the only one that has suffered in this way. Some of us get "activity-itis" and go all over the community helping others to avoid helping at home. Or perhaps we read novels or go surfing online for hours at a time.

Wisdom says that if we will "eat the frog" and get the most unpleasant things done first, the rest of the day will seem like a breeze!

Am I Over Complicating My Life?

What am I participating in out of a false sense of guilt and/or obligation that is draining me of the time and energy I need to devote to my God-given responsibilities?

These can be outside activities, online distractions, people, even possessions that require care (pets could be listed here).

Whenever I am not sure where to start, I ask my husband. He is always able to see things from a more objective perspective and helps me work through the burdens I tend to carry that are not from God.

Do I need to improve my discipline?

It takes more than soft hands and a warm heart to be a good mother; it takes self-discipline and self-sacrifice when no one is looking.

Glorious Mothering

How many times have I drug my sick, pregnant body out of bed to make sure my children had something to eat, that their clothing was clean and they knew there was security and love in the house?

Certainly life would have gone on and my children would have survived without me somehow, but it wouldn't have been the best I could have provided for them. They are not my drudgery, and they aren't my excuses, they are my gifts, and it is a privilege to serve them.

We really should see work as a good thing. Instead of avoiding it, relish it! Even if no one but God ever knows what we do behind the scenes to keep everyone comfortable, it is the minimum we owe for the great grace He has bestowed on us.

Did you know that it is the people who keep busy with work that last the longest and have the fewest illnesses?

I try and keep in mind what a blessing it is that I have a strong body, food that gives me energy, and many loved ones to care for! Those who live only for themselves are the ones to be pitied; every moment of my life is spent in wonderful *purpose*!

And, Your Big Brood Means You Have TEAMWORK!

Just think about the potentials. **Smaller children** can run errands around the house for the others, such as fetching shoes or putting away books and other items.

Middle children can cut up vegetables and fruit to have in the refrigerator for meals and snacks, bake cookies, or even write thank-you notes.

Older children can help entertain little ones, wash dishes, sort clothes, make simple dinners, clean out the car, vacuum the rugs, even mow the lawn!

For instance, one area that bogs me down is family photo organization. A little while back I had gathered 32 years' worth of family memories into one huge plastic storage bucket, but it was barely organized. It was one of those important but difficult things I kept putting off. I hated the idea of how much time it was going to take.

Then I remembered I had a crew at my disposal.

I only had to spend a few hours going through the photos and arranging them in piles. Then I handed a stack to each of my oldest daughters and asked them to put them into books I had been saving for just such an application.

Voila! Within a few hours I had four full photo albums ready and waiting for a trip down memory lane.

Here is another benefit of teamwork: When children are at least *attempting* to help, they are not running around and causing trouble!

Teaching children to help us get ahead and stay ahead will reap dividends, not only in the "now," but even after they are long grown and have lives of their own.

A hive of busy bees is much better than a cave full of people who are mind-numbed by entertainment or disgusted with their surroundings.

Glorious Mothering

Chapter 6

Weathering a Storm

Battles for the victory of right and good aren't always fought with swords and bullets. God fearing women have been "carrying on" since the beginning of time. Sarah did, and Hannah, and Abigail. Queen Esther, in order to save her people from genocide, pushed her fear to the side and stood boldly before the most powerful figure of her age.

Illness, death, financial difficulties, natural disasters, war time, and the infidelity of friends and loved ones can shake us to our foundations.

These are times when we must gird ourselves up with God's strength and keep a lid on being expressive. Our emotions must be stifled, perhaps saved for another day, or at least the wee hours of the morning when only God can hear.

When you are the spirit of the home (notice I didn't say "boss"), your light mustn't go out; it can't even flicker. You have to carry on, and you must show by your countenance all is well, even if you are quaking inside.

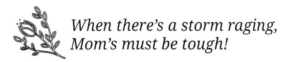

When there's a storm raging, Mom's must be tough!

Obscure wives, mothers, and grandmothers have often stood stalwart and true; patching clothes, tending the farm, and wiping away tears while offering a cheerful smile. We have been contending for our homes by keeping the fires burning in the hearth and the coffee hot on the stove. When our men have had to go off to war they could rest secure knowing we would continue to fortify the underpinnings of the family.

Like you, I haven't been a stranger to trial. I've known poverty and treachery, illness and disaster. Over the years God has imparted to me His strength and enabled me go over and through the obstacles of life. By these I have learned a few more principles which go along with the one I shared in the last chapter:

Underneath are the Everlasting Arms

When I was a child, they used to run a commercial for Nestea that showed people in oppressive heat taking the "plunge" by falling backwards into a pool of sparkling water. That's what I do when I meet with overwhelming circumstances; I fall completely into the arms of God.

I've learned that it's perfectly alright with Him if I have wobbly knees, because it's not by my strength or resolve that situations change or people are mended. I'm His little girl, and His arms lovingly embrace me when I feel helpless and overwhelmed. I can lean all the way back into Him, because He has proven His trustworthiness to me over and over again.

Stay in the Word of God

I read the Bible every day. I take it with me in my purse. I open it when I'm happy, and when I'm sad.

 I live every day from its pages, and I escape each night into its promises.

Whenever I'm so distressed that I can't even connect two thoughts in my head, I know that I can dive into the refuge of His Word and God's Spirit will begin to make sense of things for me.

Keep a Routine

Simple but true. People, especially young ones, need to know that everything will be alright. If the table is set regularly for breakfast, even if it's only a piece of toast or a small bowl of cereal, things look better.

When our hearts ache, it's the rhythm of life that keeps us from cracking to pieces and giving in to despair.

Share Carefully

There is so much professional counseling going on these days, and yet the heroines of the past were often quite solitary as they obeyed God in hard times. There's something to be said about quiet nobility and strength of character!

Some people will reach out to you who are filled with pathos, others might hug you one minute and stab you in the back the next. It's good to have a confidant, but Jesus is the Friend that sticks closer than a brother.

Pay Attention to Hope

Fill your home with messages of light. Make sure every scrap of reading material, every line of music, every minute of video viewing, is full of God's hopefulness.

I'm not advocating reading or viewing vapid drivel minus any trials, but stories of those who have faced difficulties and overcome them.

Christian biographies are hopeful and encouraging. Our all-time favorite is *The Hiding Place* by Corrie ten Boom, but there are many, many others.

We also enjoy good movies, especially ones from the past such as *I Remember Mama*, and *Sergeant York.*

Recently we have been working through a number of newer Christian films. One of our favorites is *Miracles From Heaven,* and another is *The Case for Christ.* (I think we are going to purchase the movie *The Book of Daniel* and keep it as a permanent part of our library).

Avoid Destructive Escapes

No matter how bad things get, don't fall for the lie that cheap pleasures will bring relief. The obvious ones are alcohol, drugs, sexual immorality, gambling and gossip (yes, even the magazines at the checkout in the supermarket can seem appealing when you are fighting despair, but don't even look at those poor people--pray for them, but don't engage in slander!).

Besides this, anything that's normally legitimate can become destructive when we give in to excess. Video games, reading, eating, talking on the phone and visiting, surfing the Internet, and even exercising can become traps if we're not careful to use self-control.

Don't Take it Out on Others (or Yourself)

The negative consequences from letting it all out are not worth it. Little hearts, especially, are vulnerable, and it may take a long time before you can earn back the peace of your home and trust of your family.

 Don't compound a problem by lashing out at the innocents in your life.

Crises give us practice in self-control. Instead of becoming a whining, grumbling, nasty individual, reach down deep and come up with something positive. Smile and your own cold, wintry attitude will warm up into the springtime of sweetness!

Cultivate Beauty and Enjoyment

Even in the midst of great difficulties, we need to feed our souls. I'm always amazed at how sufferers in the concentration camps of WWII found ways to enjoy themselves, even to encourage a bit of culture.

Corrie ten Boom tells of how her sister, Betsie, brightened a dank prison cell by using a red cellophane wrapper to cover the naked bulb in the room.

Americans in POW camps found ways to bring comedy and comfort to each other. One gentleman in Stalag 17 during WWII was given the title of "chef." Soldiers who were having trouble fighting hunger pangs would come up to him and he would "set the table" by describing a sumptuous dinner, complete with dessert. Prisoners who came to him for "dinner" often went away feeling full and satisfied.

Those who endured the Great Depression also knew how to create a happy atmosphere. In my grandmother's family there wasn't money for a radio, and my great grandfather would not allow any debt. So, my great grandmother would sit, turn up the coal oil lamp, and read story after story to her children at night from books they had found abandoned in barrels by the side of the road.

Sometimes they would take turns memorizing poems from these tomes and reciting them for each other. These were among my grandmother's fondest memories, and all because they were too poor to own the i-gadget of her day.

Even in this technological age it is still fun to have a family sing-along, dance around to some rousing music, play Mad Libs, play board games, or enjoy reading aloud

Glorious Mothering

(a favorite in our family).

We are such a goofy crew at our house that it doesn't take much to get us going, and before long we are all grabbing our sides in the blessed pain of too much laughter!

And Don't Forget Handicrafts

Did you know they offer knitting classes in hospitals where mothers spend hour after hour worrying over children with debilitating or terminal illnesses?

 Stitchery calms us because it gives us something productive to do with our hands as well as our minds.

I have often found this to be true for myself. During a time when my husband was unemployed I found great comfort in crocheting about 15 doilies and hand-sewing just as many dolls out of old socks and bits of cloth.

Actively Praise and Thank God

Every day we're met with the realities of our physical world. We awaken to bills unpaid, or bodily pain, or the loneliness of a broken heart. All of these things conspire to bring us down, to keep us from believing that God can and will be our Comforter and Deliverer.

The devil likes to puff himself up in our minds, to make us believe that darkness is strong enough to eclipse the power of God in our lives.

The best way to combat his lies is to magnify the Lord; to remind ourselves of His great power, of His love, of His kindness towards mankind, and even of His righteous justice.

(I encourage you to read all of 2 Chronicles 20, the story will really bless you.)

Read the Psalms aloud, listen to them on CD, or sing them out for yourself. Play praise music throughout the day. Find a hymnal and sing as many of the songs out loud as you can. Fill your home with the praises of God and practice thanking Him, even if you stub your toe!

Stand on Top of It All

One of the most important things we need to remember is that this world is not our home.

God can pull us up so we can stand on the peak of a problem and look down on it instead of seeing it as a looming mountain blocking our path.

Christ has risen indeed, and when we rest with Him, seated at the right hand of God, we can look down on our fears and torments and see them for the imposter's they truly are.

Here are some scriptures for meditation when you are going through a storm:

And we know that all things work together for good to them that love God, to them who are the called according to his purpose..
Romans 8:28

My soul fainteth for thy salvation: but I hope in thy word.
Psalm 119:81

She is clothed with strength and dignity; she can laugh at the days to come.
Proverbs 31:25

Now when Daniel knew that the writing was signed, he went into his house; and his windows being open in his chamber toward Jerusalem, he kneeled upon his knees three times a day, and prayed, and gave thanks before his God, as he did aforetime.
Daniel 6:10

He will cover you with his feathers, and under his wings you will find refuge; his faithfulness will be your shield and rampart.
Psalm 91:4

Finally, brethren, whatsoever things are true, whatsoever things are honest, whatsoever things are just, whatsoever things are pure, whatsoever things are lovely, whatsoever things are of good report; if there be any virtue, and if there be any praise, think on these things.
Philippians 4:8

To appoint unto them that mourn in Zion, to give unto them beauty for ashes, the oil of joy for mourning, the garment of praise for the spirit of heaviness; that they might be called trees of righteousness, the planting of the LORD, that he might be glorified.
Isaiah 61:3

Let us walk honestly, as in the day; not in rioting and drunkenness, not in chambering and wantonness, not in strife and envying.
Romans 13:13

And when he had consulted with the people, he appointed singers unto the Lord, and that should praise the beauty of holiness, as they went out before the army, and to say, Praise the Lord; for his mercy endureth for ever.
2 Chronicles 20:21

Now thanks be unto God, which always causeth us to triumph in Christ, and maketh manifest the savour of his knowledge by us in every place.
2 Chronicles 2:14

Glorious Mothering

Chapter 7

Streamlining

Much of the conflict we experience at home does not have a deep, spiritual cause. A great amount of the emotional distress we deal with can be traced back to one culprit; clutter!

Clutter is not just a crowded row of figurines on a shelf or a stack of unread mail on the counter; it is anything added that actually subtracts from our lives.

This can include:

• Craft supplies

• Toys

• Complicated machines

• Complicated schedules

• "Bells and whistles"

• Electronic media

- Entertainment

- Furnishings

- Kitchen gadgets

- Activities

- People

- Curriculum

Take Time to Reevaluate

Let's face it; "extras" aren't always *extra*. How many things do you find yourself sighing over, or stumbling over, or worrying over without stopping to ask why?

Is it really necessary to keep every picture a child creates and place it on the fridge? Who says our children must have five pairs of shoes a piece? Is it really wise to try and fit 8000 square feet of furniture into a 1000 square foot house? How many grocery bags do I really need to save? How many old toothbrushes will I really use to clean around the toilet?

Will my children be stunted if we are not running from one activity to the other all week long? Will the church close its doors if we are not there every single meeting?

Will we cease to exist if we do not have enough i-gadgets? Will our children really go crazy if we don't allow them to play video games all-day-long?

Stop Comparing and Start Living

When I began mothering I was young and impressionable and certain that everyone else who ran around constantly had the right idea. My friends would talk of how involved they were at church, the elaborate birthday parties they threw, the thrilling vacations they took, etc.

Somehow, when I tried to keep up with what I perceived everyone else was doing I became a mess. It didn't take long to realize that my children didn't need to have every experience and every possession every other child had if it meant a "mommy melt-down."

 Trying to live according to everyone else's standards made me a hypocrite; griping and fussing in private, but pasting on a smile in public just to impress others.

That is why I decided long ago to only keep those things and activities that added value. I call this "Streamlining."

Examples:

- For birthdays we have a few gifts, a cake, and sing happy birthday. We also add in the priceless--we talk all day about what a blessing the birthday boy or girl is and share happy memories.

- Kitchen gadgets are at a minimum. Basic pots, pans, etc. do most of the jobs better, anyway.

- While we are all quite savvy technology-wise, we don't own the latest and greatest. We use only what is functional and economical and ignore the rest.

- My washing machine has a control panel with more buttons than the space shuttle, but I only use two cycles.

- My refrigerator also has a control panel with more neon than Las Vegas at night, but I only pay attention to what kinds of ice I want; chipped or cubed!

- My morning routine fits nicely into a wicker case, and I adhere to a "capsule" wardrobe. I own 4 pairs of regular shoes according to the seasons (with one pair each of dress shoes in white, black and brown).

- I have four tabs that I keep track of on my browser; the others I add or subtract as necessary.

- Even though I have a business presence online, I keep my activity there within boundaries.

- We have four breakfast choices, lunch is sandwiches or leftovers, and there are about eight different dishes that I plan for dinner, rotated as needed (as long as these bases are covered, we are free to add something special if we want to).

- Outside activities are very few; only the ones where we are truly contributing and learning from.

- I floundered around for years homeschooling with

different methods and materials until I discovered the most direct route: Eclectic Education materials (like the McGuffey Readers, Ray's Arithmetics, and Long's Language), "living" books, and notebooking.

- I love beautiful things, but even these can become burdens. I tend to think that a few fabulous decorations are much better than a horde of ticky-tacky curios and mementos.

You Can't Streamline Until You Have Purged

In fact, writing this chapter is reminding me of all of the things I need to go through very soon, such as...

- **Glasses and dishes.** You know, the ones that are chipped, stained, awkward, or simply *ugly*!

- **Shoes.** Season changes are a good times to go through and check the condition and sizes of shoes, then keep a list of who needs what for those spontaneous garage-sale or thrifting times.

- **Clothes.** This also comes with the seasonal change. We pass our clothes down as much as possible, but there are times when things just wear out (or we have kept things that are awful looking in the hopes that hanging them in the closet will somehow improve them).

- **Papers.** This is a big one for me, since I tend to dislike going through piles of bills and the like, and filing seems like running in place.

- **Food.** Have you ever bought something like a can of lima beans and kept it for five years before finally deciding your family will never eat them? Well, purging helps me come to grips with the fact that: 1) spending money on food my family will not eat is wasteful, and 2) if I ever make a mistake and purchase something distasteful, I should have the sense to donate it before the "best by" date so that someone else can enjoy it.

Preparation is Helpful

Purging is tremendous work! So, in order to do a good job, I have to get in the mood. Oftentimes I have used the Internet to spur me on by researching and reading everything I can on decluttering and organizing. I also have a playlist on YouTube labeled "Cleanin' Music" which is lined up with get-going tunes.

Making lists of goals and directions (for me and everyone helping) can invigorate me as well.

When I am sufficiently charged up, I grab my general planning pages, get containers and bags ready, and hand out assignments to all of my "volunteers"!

Keep That Rock Rollin'

Some people argue that you can streamline in small snatches of time, but I tend to need a few days in which I dig in and don't stop until I get to the bottom of it all (my poor husband reads the signs and finds a place to hide when I begin a deep-clean session).

Glorious Mothering

About half-way through it's easy to run out of steam, and this is especially true for my "crew" of helpers. This is when I bring out some motivators; treats such as packaged granola bars or cookies, or maybe the announcement of a special outing once everything is accomplished.

Or, I might show them some videos on YouTube to infuse new enthusiasm for our task.

If my children are really, really burnt out, I will send them all off to entertain each other, either assigning the older children to take the younger ones on a walk to the park or to sit down and watch a well-earned picture show while I continue to work (while I appreciate the opportunity to train the children in keeping things up, having unhampered time to move quickly without interruption is a treat to me).

Use Purging to Revamp Systems and Spaces

As I am decluttering I am thinking of new and better ways to formulate routines. This is when I take a sore spot in our daily lives and look at it from all sides. Maybe we need to change the procedures we use get ready in the morning. Perhaps reordering the bathing sequence is the solution. Are we adding too much into our mealtimes? Is there a more efficient way to clean up after dinner? Is there at better way to stow personal hygiene gear?

I am also considering where we place things. Is it better to have towels hung up in the bathrooms or in stacks in the hall closet? Would it be better to have the toys in the bedrooms or in a central, out-of-the-way, place? Is the flow of traffic from the dining room to the kitchen being hindered by excess furnishings?

A wondrous side-benefit is that during this whole process I am accomplishing a lot of cleaning as well, since we are getting into places that otherwise would be hard to reach. We are vacuuming under couches and beds, wiping off high shelves, getting in the nooks, crannies, and corners of closets and cupboards, etc.

This not only cuts down on stress and makes for a more peaceful family life, but it leads to a great sense of accomplishment.

The point of streamlining is to creating and honing systems so that your family knows what to expect, and where, and when.

I am often gently amused when I hear the current mantra of "empowerment" for women outside the home. I have worked in some powerful, interesting jobs, but homemaking is by far the most gratifying of all!

Chapter 8

Getting Ahead

I grew up with only one sister, so I didn't understand just how "dynamic" life would be when I decided to trust God and have a big family.

But as we grew and there were loads of people who interacted, especially when these people were tiny, there seemed to be one emergency after another, some days with no lull time in-between. At times it felt so overwhelming that I was tempted to take a *permanent* break!

I know there are many moms who feel the same way.

A Sad Story

One dear woman wrote to me and explained just how awful things can get. Her house and family were in such horrible disarray that basic human needs were going unmet and at one time her children had been snatched away by the authorities. Even after her children were returned she was unable to cope, choosing to lie in bed and hide instead of doing the wash and feeding her children.

I was, of course, compassionate towards this mother,

but I was also honest and gave her a proverbial kick in the pants (which she thanked me for).

I don't believe she started out as a rotten homemaker. She had the same ambitions we all have; she wanted to have a clean, peaceful, orderly home in which everyone's needs were met and love flowed freely.

Her steps into the dark abyss were taken slowly and steadily until they all began to snowball. All of her "un-dones" began to work on her mind until she was actually physically ill at the thought of her many burdens.

This left her without energy to tackle even one of them successfully.

To be sure, she felt as though she was chasing an unobtainable dream; always running behind, always thwarted, until she was unable to keep up and fell helpless in the dust.

There is Hope!

Life as the mother of many people has its challenges, but, as we have been discussing, they do not have to be overwhelming. By making positive choices, we can overcome and pull ourselves back from the plunge into despair.

By keeping certain keys in mind, we can live productive, joyful, loving lives, no matter what circumstances we are facing.

These keys are:

Faith

and

Getting Ahead.

Faith

At its essence, the difference between a woman who is haggard and overcome and the woman who is hopeful and ready for life is one thing: believing in a God who is there and who wants to bless His children.

There is no way to *over*emphasize this one principle (which is why I keep mentioning it). Our reliance in faith makes all the difference, from the ways we respond to our children to the ways we keep our kitchens clean.

> Therefore if any man be in Christ, he is a new creature: old things are passed away; behold, all things are become new.
> 2 Corinthians 5:17

Being "saved" is just the beginning of the miracles that God wants to continually do in our lives. As soon as we believe He replaces our old nature with His new one. Then it is simply a matter of training our mind, will, and emotions to come under the control of that born-again spirit.

And how is this done? In Romans 12, verse two, we are told that in order to escape the tendencies of our old selves we need to renew our minds, and the way we renew our minds is to meditate on His Word.

For me, this has meant that I have:

1. Set aside specific times for reading and prayer--not always in the morning, but oftentimes during afternoon quiet time.

2. Utilized modern technology by playing recorded scripture and Biblical teaching throughout the day; while washing dishes, folding laundry, running errands, etc.

3. Been disciplining my mind to think only those thoughts in line with Philippians 4:8:

> Finally, brethren, whatever things are true, whatever things are noble, whatever things are just, whatever things are pure, whatever things are lovely, whatever things are of good report, if there is any virtue and if there is anything praiseworthy—meditate on these things.

I have found that there is less tension because I am not as worried. While I am training my mind, my emotions follow, and I find that I can head off stress that would cause me to become angry or frustrated with the ones I love and serve.

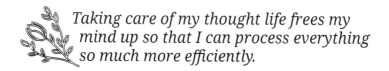

Taking care of my thought life frees my mind up so that I can process everything so much more efficiently.

Getting Ahead

Being unprepared has been the cause of much evil in the world. It is one thing to be overcome by things that we have no control over, it is another to live without prudence so that even simple events of life become disasters.

"Getting ahead" means planning and preparing in advance. It means that I don't have to run to the store every morning for breakfast food. It means that I am not constantly digging through piles of unwashed or unfolded laundry to find a work shirt for my husband. It means that I am not spending two hours looking for a pencil when it is time to homeschool my children.

Getting ahead means to think ahead and to do ahead.

Of course, there are occasions when people are ill and the laundry piles up, but there are ways to keep from being totally overcome even in *these* times.

Plan for Contingencies

This means I keep an inventory of supplies that will be needed in case of minor injury or illness, such as a plastic case filled with items for bandaging wounds and dealing with splinters, stingers, upset stomachs and other aches and pains...

I also try and maintain a pantry stocked with raw materials which can be used to form frugal and delicious meals such as meats, flour, vegetables and spices. In this way I am rarely caught off-guard when it comes to food preparation.

Along with this I keep a running list of possible meals based on what I have accumulated, always attempting to use perishable items first.

As for homeschooling, I purchase the basic supplies we will need at discounted prices during the back to school sales in late summer and then portion them out during the rest of the year. I also try and have a loose plan of what we are going to study in the next few months so I can make sure and have the books and materials we will need on hand.

Give Plans Substance

One very important way that I "get ahead" is to utilize quiet moments to make plans on paper. Oftentimes it has been as a baby has been nursing and sleeping on my lap that I will grab a small notepad and scribble down a list of ideas in a mind map. I will often include materials I might need (such as paint or hardware if it is a home project) and even the specific assignments for the children who will be helping (I consider home projects to be an essential part of their education).

Having a plan on paper has saved my sanity many

times, especially since I try and have my mind free so I can pay attention "in the moment."

I have found that if I don't have a written, concrete list my mind becomes overloaded and I get off track and lose all of my hard work! It is so refreshing to pull out a notebook and find things spelled-out plainly so that all I have to do is implement them.

Put Things in Place Before the "Crunch" Times

Crunches are things like church day, going on a trip, having guests over, holidays, and family meals.

This is when multiple details must come together at one time in order for there to be a continuous, harmonious flow. Sort of like how all of the

I ask myself, "How many things can I accomplish before bedtime that will bless me when I awaken in the morning?"

instruments in a symphony orchestra must play together when performing something as lovely as a Strauss waltz.

One way I do this is by thinking about tomorrow the night before.

Here are some that I can think of:

- Clean the kitchen

- Vacuum the floors

- Pick up the bedrooms

- Fold and put the laundry away

- Set out the clothes for the next day

- Plan the next-day's meals, set out breakfast, prepare "lunch packs"

- Fill up the coffee maker so that it will automatically start in the morning

- Plan homeschooling for the next day

Use the Team

The almost magical thing about large family life is that I don't have to perform all of these tasks by myself! I have a set list of chores each family member does before bed while I sit and plan for homeschooling and meals, then I make sure they are done well and add some of my own touches before I trip off to bed.

Only in His Strength

Of course, there are times when even the best of plans are interrupted, and this is where faith is exercised. If we don't learn to trust that God will help us no matter how our plans pan out, we are going to increase our stress instead of reducing it!

However, if we are in the habit of keeping ahead wherever possible, we have less trouble getting back on track when things return to "normal" (whatever that means!).

Chapter 9

Making Children Behave

When we began homeschooling we thought we were escaping the woolly beast of negative peer dependence (you know, the "blind-leading-the-blind" phenomenon). Our children would be protected from such things as drug use, bullying, and teen fornication. By and large, we did keep our kids safe from a lot of what the rest of the world considers "normal" problems.

However, we also thought that homeschooling would make all the *rest* of parenting easier. Our kids were not supposed to have bad attitudes, bad habits, or bad breath.

What we didn't know is that in looking to create perfection, we were instead forced to face our own *im*perfections.

You probably know what I am talking about. Even though things are infinitely more civilized in your snug little home, you still struggle almost daily with your own unruly "students." This shouldn't be strange. After all, children are just young *people*, and we as people struggle with nastiness, stubbornness, and all sorts of negative evils simply because we are all *sinners.*

It is something we don't want to share on Instagram, something that we rarely admit to others. It is a hard truth that we do battle with the same distractedness and outbursts as all parents since Adam and Eve.

Familiarity Breeds Contempt

Public schooled students often comply because they don't want to be embarrassed, but homeschooled children don't have anyone to impress, so they can let their emotions flow freely. This makes them more prone to bad attitudes and manipulative behavior because they don't have to worry about what every one will think of them when they whine, complain, cry or throw temper tantrums.

Of course, they wouldn't be using these tactics if they weren't effective. So many times we become duped into thinking, "If I give in, then I will have peace!" But we fail to realize such a peace is only temporary, and by giving in we are encouraging more of the same.

If they don't want to do a worksheet of addition problems, they only need to sigh or groan and Mom will renege, especially if they are astute enough to clue in to her desire to give them a "natural" education. They know they can bop their younger siblings and cause chaos whenever they are bored with copywork or would rather be digging in the sand in the back yard.

Passion Must Be Ruled by Discipline

Now, I am a great advocate of more delight-led learning. This is something I emphasize over and over in my writing and the subject matter I choose to share on all my social media.

But there is a balance.

We may not follow any "scope and sequence" as laid out by the educational establishment, but this does not mean that our learning is one massive, monstrous, boisterous, chaotic free-for-all. If it were, I would not be able to type this right now because my arms would be wrapped up in a straight-jacket and I would be sitting in a padded room!

When I started out homeschooling my own children I was not ready for the battles I would have to face. Instead of insisting and pushing hard enough to get past the resistance, I gave in on a regular basis. Sometimes it was as if I was validating my own tendency towards slothfulness by allowing them to pull the wool over my eyes. I also allowed my sloppy, sentimental view of love cloud my judgment.

Every homeschooling mother MUST have order, and that order must be gained at the expense of one's own comfort.

As I began to mature I realized the more noble side of love, the side painted with self-sacrifice; willing to risk offense in order to gain finer things. In keeping with these realizations my parenting changed for the better.

As I moved away from an emotion-based love there was more calm, more compliance, and a better learning atmosphere for all. Eventually I began to put together a formula of sorts that I could revisit at any time and apply like a salve on a wound.

Whenever we began to experience resistance and bad attitudes, all I had to do was apply the same wisdom and methods and we were back on track again.

I've actually had to apply this formula numerous times over the years as a constant new "crop" of young people come into maturity.

Although it would take volumes to explain every aspect of our parenting remedy, here are a few of the high points:

Use the Word.

Since God is the Parent of us all, studying His ways and His intents is better than reading a thousand books on parenting from anyone else.

> The rod and reproof give wisdom: but a child left to himself bringeth his mother to shame.
> Proverbs 29:15

> All scripture given by inspiration of God, and profitable for doctrine, for reproof, for correction, for instruction in righteousness.
> 2 Timothy

84

Proverbs is the most specific source for basic instruction in wisdom and righteousness, but only a thorough study of the whole Bible will yield a complete picture of God's type of parenting. I try and have scripture keys at the ready whenever it is time for correction, such as:

> Love worketh no ill to his neighbor: therefore love is the fulfilling of the law.
> Romans 13:10

Which is terrific to use when one child is abusing another in any way.

I also try and teach these principles deliberately daily to our children so they will be very familiar with them as we bring them up.

Gain the Child's Full Attention.

For me, eye contact is a must. Jesus said the eyes are gateways to the soul. When I take the time to capture their attention it takes much less time to correct or advise.

Be Fully Engaged

Especially in our crazy, busy age, this is one of the most difficult points. Gadgets, phone calls, social media and entertainment all vie for our attention. We need to keep in mind that parenting is just like the stock market; we can only expect a return on what we are willing to invest.

Do we desire well-behaved, respectful, children? Then we must be willing to give them their due attention. Neither the computer, nor the DVD player, nor the preschool program will be able to perform the job that God has laid at our feet. Even if the pastor himself should call up and ask to divert our attention for some other "good" cause–we must make the better choice and tend to the little church members in our homes!

Here are some important things to keep in mind:

- We not only need to discipline our children, we need to discipline ourselves.

- We need to be respected, so we must become respectable.

- We need to have attention, so we must pay attention.

- We need to have instant response, so we must be available and responsive.

Beware of the "Monologue"

There is certainly a place for "lecturing," but too many of us rely on the wagging of our tongues to do the job of correction. This is the most inefficient of methods.

While we are called upon to reason with our children (reproof), it is a sign of laziness and neglect when a parent continually harps on the same subject or gives numerous "warnings" without taking action.

Our own children have been known to purposely

encourage us to talk about some principle or story of illustration (remember, we are older and have a lot of these to share!) so that they can postpone (or help us to forget) correction. They know that if they can get us talking our vehemence will be dissipated and we may forget why we were correcting them altogether!

> Chasten thy son while there is hope, and let not thy soul spare for his crying.
> Proverbs 19:18

Make Correction Meaningful.

There are just certain things which can only be learned through the application of the unpleasant; and these means have to cause a measured amount of pain in one form or another. If you are too reluctant to cause your child discomfort, you will cause him great harm.

A child that has never had his will trained in this way is being prepared for a life full of misery, for everyone whom God loves receives His correction, and those who have been trained to recognize it are the most blessed.

> There is a knot tied between the soul and sin, a true lover's knot; they two became one flesh. It is true of ourselves, it is true of our children, whom we have begotten in our own likeness. O God! Thou knowest this foolishness...correction is necessary to the cure of it. It will not be got out by fair means and gentle methods; there must be strictness and severity, and that which will cause grief. Children need to be

corrected, and kept under discipline, by their parents;
and we all need to be corrected by our heavenly
Father (Heb. 12:6, 7), and under the correction we
must stroke down folly and kiss the rod.
-Matthew Henry's A Commentary on the Whole Bible,
Proverbs 22:15.

Praise and Reward Good Behavior

It has been said that one critical remark should be
balanced by ten positive ones. So, while doling out the
correction, make sure and pile on the encouragement
where appropriate (not empty flattery).

Here are some words and phrases to use:

"You are such a blessing, I am so glad God gave you to
me!"

"Good job!"

"You did that exactly right!"

"You work so well that it gives me joy just to watch
you!"

"I am so impressed by your good attitude; keep it up!"

"You cheer everyone up by your smile and happy
ways!" etc.

Even if you don't see a lot of positives in your child at
the moment, speaking positive words into his/her life
is planting of seeds in faith. Continue the practice even

when you don't observe a lot of change at first, and you will be rejoicing at the harvest you will reap in due time!

Here is a fun exercise; one morning, instead of correcting for a bad job, start passing out m&m candies to anyone you "catch" doing something correctly–I do this every once-in-a-while and it is so much fun!

Take Time to Instruct Them

When we come across misbehavior that is not incidental but recurring, we put our children through a two-part course. First, we explain what they are doing and why it is wrong and harmful, then we show them what they are doing so they can see for themselves.

The first step can be tricky sometimes. While we want to drive home the significance of their infraction, we don't want to make them feel attacked so they shut down and tune out. Often times telling a story from the past helps a lot here. This way we show them that their problem is not strange and, with God's help and some diligence on their part, it can be overcome.

The second part, showing them, is much easier and can even be a lot of fun. These days we can even turn to something like YouTube to show them videos of kids acting up so they can see just how silly, sad, or destructive it is.

Our favorite way, however, is through "role-play." This is where we set up situations and put on a little show so our children can see how awful they look when they misbehave. Humor is a big part of this activity, which really helps drive the idea home (this is all done in a spirit of love and acceptance, not as an opportunity to belittle them).

Then we call on them to show us how a person *should* act, and we have them practice a couple of times to make sure the message sinks in.

Act in Justice

Young people, especially boys, care deeply about justice. If we are inconsistent, if our children don't know whether we are going to be strict or soft about misbehavior, they lose respect and then shut down.

But if they know there is a standard, they settle down and gain respect for us.

One thing that can help is to come up with a list of possible infractions and their corresponding consequences. Then, when something comes up, everyone will know just what should be done. Not only does this keep children feeling more secure, but it also keeps us, the parents, from using anger as a correction tool. While how riled we are over an infraction might change from time-to-time, the proscribed correction does not, so that no one can complain some children are being favored while others are being targeted.

In the past I have added some graphics and then printed out and posted these on the refrigerator for everyone to see.

Teach Respect

This is another one of those things that do not come naturally to us but are essential to living good lives. Responding quickly when called, answering with an appropriate "Yes, Ma'am," or "Yes, Sir," and questioning without dishonoring those in authority are among the skills that must be taught.

If a child fails to respond promptly to me, I require they "practice" coming quickly 10 times. If they can't come quickly, they are to call out, "Coming, Mom (or Dad)" as loud as is necessary for me to hear him (we have a large house). This, also, must be practiced in order for it to become automatic.

When being addressed, they are to be in a listening posture, not staring at the ceiling or looking into a gadget.

They are not allowed to "tease" with questions and reasons why they cannot comply. Instead, they are taught how to make a respectful appeal via the role-play method mentioned above.

Use Chores to Gain Character.

I like to tell my children a tale of two people. One was highly educated and immensely talented. The other was only slightly talented and barely educated.

The first man was lazy, capricious, and self-interested. The second man was hard-working, single-minded and fiercely determined to gain character instead of giving in to his emotional whims.

None of us know the name of the first man, because all of his talent and education went to waste.

But the name of the second man we know well. He has been called George Washington, Benjamin Franklin, and George Washington Carver, among many others that are notable and worthy.

The point? At the end of the day, hard work will get you farther than talent!

Helping out at home trains the temper and builds the body. Chores help children learn perseverance and compassion for others.

Working together builds family bonds. If a child learns to be helpful at home they have more of a connection to the people there and feel vested in what happens to them. Family projects where everyone takes a part fill young people with a sense of belonging and satisfaction.

In addition to all the other benefits mentioned, having children help with the responsibilities of family life gives us opportunities to diagnose problems and deal with them before they become an element of a child's personality and character.

This is why chores are never optional. Everyone has a specific list of responsibilities, but it doesn't stop there. Each individual also knows they may be called upon to go

Glorious Mothering

above and beyond what is written on the list.

Dealing With Push-back

Do we ever experience complaining and shirking? Certainly, but only temporarily. This is because of a two-fold response:

1. If a child complains or grumbles that something is too much, they get double the work.

For instance, dinner clean up is a team effort because we have found that "many hands make light work." However, younger children can sometimes whine and strike up arguments with others, even if their job is very easy. I have found the best way to straighten them up in a hurry is to have them clean the entire kitchen by themselves!

2. If their assigned work is done slovenly, they have to do it over until it is up to standards.

For instance, if a bed is wrinkly, the covers are taken off and it must be made again from scratch. This usually only has to be done one time before a child gets the picture!

(Of course, all of what I have described here is done according to age and ability. Only a wicked, foolish person would expect tiny children to do more than they are capable of, or to expect the children to do the work of the parents.)

A young person who refuses to respond quickly when

called, who constantly talks-back, and who is not held accountable for sloppy, half-hearted work will be a constant drain. He will make the teaching of every subject a headache for the whole family, and he will be more likely to reap a harvest of heartache in life.

Contrarily, a home full of children, although imperfect, who understand what is expected and the consequences of trespassing on the rules and standards set forth by caring, loving parents, is a happy one indeed!

Chapter 10

Keeping Track by Herding

I find sheep dogs to be one of the most amazing domesticated animals on earth. Just one of these canines can take a bunch of scattered sheep and unify them so that they flow as one body.

This is what I have learned to do with my own little flock.

It all began many years ago, when I had a LOT of little children to take around with me grocery shopping, to the bank, and so on. It may have been pride, or The Golden Rule, or a mixture of both, but I knew that I did not want my children to be a menace wherever we went. I determined we were not going to be looked at as "that" large family.

The only problem was how to go about keeping my children in line...

Give Them Structure

After prayer, thought, and observation, this is one of the conclusions I came to:

> *Children often cause trouble because they do not know what they are supposed to be doing with themselves.*

We assume they know, but this is where we are wrong. If you think about it, they are sort of like aliens from another planet. All of the things we take for granted every day are totally unfamiliar to them.

When they are thrust into strange situations and we do not help them know what they are supposed to do they will begin to try and figure it out for themselves, and this is where we have problems. (The fear of the unknown causes most adults to react in some way; imagine being four years old and trying to make sense of a bunch of new circumstances all at once!)

However, if we give them clear directions and boundaries, they will settle down and work within them, just as the sheepdog does with his flock.

So, I developed strategies for outings. Before we went, there was a "talk" about what we were going to experience and what the expectations were. This way they were able to adjust their enthusiasm and energy either up (for a play-date) or down (for a visit with an elderly person).

Next, I provided my children "physicality" to their

surroundings. Instead of allowing them to feel like they were dangling in thin air I tried to find something they could touch or grab onto, such as a wall or counter.

This actually saved their lives on a few occasions, such as when getting out of the car on a crowded street or parking lot. I trained them to stand against the car until I was able to situate the baby, grab a cart, etc. instead of rushing out the door and into traffic!

No matter where we went together, they were a group, and they moved as a group, even to the restroom.

If we were at the store and they were walking, they were required to "glue" to the cart by clasping some part of it. If we were standing in a line at the bank, they either "glued" to me or to each other. To keep touching to a minimum, they were required to keep their hands either behind their backs or in their pockets (as a reminder I would say, "Look with your eyes, not your fingers.")

Instead of constantly chasing them and apologizing to others for their antics, I beamed as they were bathed in the compliments of onlooking strangers for their respectful, polite behavior.

No, we weren't *that* large family, we were THAT large family!

Herding on the Homefront

This was such a successful experiment that I applied it

at home, too. Like a sheep dog, I have learned to move my little flock fluidly through the events of each day.

First of all, I have trained my children to "hear my voice." Just as the sheepdog expects the sheep to follow his cues, I make announcements as to what we are doing next. Now, this may change from day-to-day, but I expect that when these changes take place everyone will adapt.

For instance, this morning I am having them do their personal hygiene before our morning meeting, yesterday we had our morning meeting first, the day before we started our chores and then broke for our morning meeting.

It is all according to the need and the circumstance.

And this is how our days go. I announce the next band of activities, and then have everyone flow in that vein. (Of course, the children are allowed to ask what's going to happen next, too.)

Just as any good shepherd would expect, there are no stragglers. Unless there is an announced "free time," each individual is expected to participate in the activity of the group or in the support of the group.

There are many benefits to this type of system:

- It keeps a lid on mess, since I can make sure everything is tidied up after an activity.

- It cuts down on confusion, since I am not trying to

keep track of numerous activities at the same time.

- Waste is minimized because I am able to supervise more, and it is less noisy.

What Will the Children Think?

In order to explain this I will need to resort to a movie comparison. We own both the new and the older versions of the movie, *Yours, Mine and Ours* which attempt to portray what life is like in "blended" large families, that is, where children of two families are joined into a new one.

The newer film depicts two distinct types of parenting styles–one that is free-wheeling and driven by creativity and life "in the moment" with disorganization and mess being a part of everyday life, and another that is orderly and clean with a military influence.

I was sure my children would favor the free-wheeling type of family life, but, to my great astonishment, they were disgusted by it.

They loved the orderliness of the military family, and even told me we should strive to be more like it! (And this was coming from kids who love to create and draw, play music, etc.)

Of course, within any system there should be time for individual expression. Any parent who does not deliberately make space and time for her children to be alone as individuals is gravely mistaken, but without boundaries the situation very easily turns into an ugly, dysfunctional monster.

Order Brings Rest

There is security in orderliness; in having three meals a day and routines or in knowing where to find your socks in a hurry!

This has not come easily to me. My initial tendency was to see everything through the eyes of a creative visionary, which can lead to over stimulation and exhaustion.

Through the years I have learned to tune-in to my stress level. If I find I am losing my enthusiasm and feeling pinched, it usually means I am trying to do too many things at once. I immediately stop everything and reassess, praying for wisdom, of course. I then apply my own prescriptions as outlined in the beginning of this book until I once again sense the peace of God, both personally and in the atmosphere of my home.

Less is More

This means we can't do everything; we can't have all the "experiences" our little hearts may desire. But we can enjoy the few things we do to their fullest and enjoy each other at the same time instead of feeling fractured and isolated while pursuing 15 different expressions of self-interest.

Even as the older children are with us less often due to outside demands, such as jobs, activities, and/or deadlines, I still expect the younger bunch to follow along

Glorious Mothering

as they always have. In this way the younger children do not hamper the older ones, and the older ones are considerate of the flow of our household and encourage their younger siblings to cooperate. It may sound funny, but even the older children choose to do things together as much as possible.

For instance, the two grown graphic artists in our home sit next to each other, often with a gathering of younger siblings as well, while they "art," encouraging and consulting with each other as they go along.

Following this principle has created a better cohesion. It has given us a family identity that wouldn't have been possible had we all been scattered all of the time. The house stays cleaner, and the positive interaction has become more lively as the children age.

Sometimes maybe a little *too* lively, but I still count it as a blessing!

Chapter 11

Harness the Potential Energy in Your Family for God's Glory

Our God is a God of order (1 Corinthians 14:33). Whatever He creates is formed perfectly, instantly. When God placed Adam and Eve in the Garden of Eden, it was perfect; no dust bunnies, no trash dumps, no broken-down cars on the front lawn.

Then sin happened, and everything changed. All of a sudden, there was destruction and disorganization. Creation began groaning under the weight of it all, and so did we.

While it is not pleasant, all of this fighting against the weeds and the trash in our lives is God's gift to us. It keeps us humble, and it hampers us from having unlimited time and energy to carry out all kinds of dastardly deeds (just think of what a drug dealer or despot could accomplish without having to deal with natural hindrances).

Big Family, Big Problems?

Obviously, as a mom of 15 children I fight the fight against disorder daily. Where there are many people (especially children) there is always that potential for chaos. This is what people expect, what they see in their minds when they think of a huge family.

The remake of the movie *Cheaper by the Dozen* includes humorous examples. One scene in particular shows the whole family going through their morning routines when chaos erupts, mostly having to do with a pet frog. Somehow the breakfast table turns into a disaster zone, with splattered cereal and broken glassware. Then the bus horn sounds and all of the children rush off, leaving mom to clean up the aftermath.

Real large family life includes moments like these. There are times when everything goes wrong all at once; when the washer breaks down in the middle of an ice storm and everyone has the stomach flu, or when six children come down with the chicken pox in the middle of moving (true story).

This is life on planet earth.

More Risk, More Help

If a married couple has opened their hearts to God to receive children, then they are in a very privileged position.

Jesus said that when we receive a little child in His name we receive Him. And in receiving Him, we receive all that He is about: His comfort, His strength, His guidance, His covering, and His provision. If we abandon ourselves to this ministry to children in our homes, we are even in a better stead. There are some implied blessings that go along with people who are surrendered and trust implicitly in Gods provision and protection. Large families can tap into these blessings anytime, anywhere.

If large families experience magnified problems, they also enjoy help that goes above and beyond what normal humans experience.

The Bible Tells Me So

We have a picture of this in the nation of Israel in the Old Testament. Many, many times they were threatened by enemies (usually the Philistines) and overwhelming odds, but as soon as they cried out to God He showed up. He delivered them repeatedly, and often without any help on their part!

Oftentimes the trials, the messes, and the chaos we face in our home lives are like the Philistines. These menaces threaten us on our borders. They want to drive in and take over, but when we cry out to God, He rushes in with reinforcements and helps us to fight and overcome!

Many Hands Make Light Work

And here's another great encouragement to consider: The very people that make the messes and increase the chaos are also the people who can work and help, even build and fix.

At times we have been 15 or more people eating

around our table, which means 15 people capable of helping out in one way or another. These individuals can cut carrots, clean floors, stir gravy, flip pancakes, set the table, etc. Then, when the meal is over, just as many people can clean everything up (of course, having everyone help all at once is just as awful as not having anyone to help at all, so this is where Mom steps in with a clipboard, and sometimes a whistle!).

When I had five bedrooms, four bathrooms, three living areas, and two offices to keep clean, I also had an army of people to vacuum, to dust, to scrub toilets and tubs, and to take out the trash. On "heavy" washing day, for example, when we changed sheets and towels, I would have approximately six large baskets of clothing to fold, but I also had at least six pairs of helping hands to get the job done!

Tackle it Like a Team

When we moved into our last house we had 12 children ranging from eight-months-old to 19 years old. It was new construction, which meant that the yard was nothing more than some sand speckled with weeds. My husband and I knew that our kids needed a place to play, so we purchased a wooden play fort kit (complete with swings), some railroad ties, and a load of sand from a local landscaping company.

Because we are a mega family, we rallied and conquered! What takes most folks weeks to accomplish we did in one day. Dad and the boys took care of building the fort, and the girls and I put the ties around the base, filled them in with the sand, then painted them a color to match the fort.

Grandpa had been invited to help and was absolutely amazed; within a few hours the whole project was completed, including the painting!

When we trust the power of His Holy Spirit in our lives to help us conquer the chaos and destruction sin brought upon us, we are working the answer to the prayer, "Thy Kingdom come, Thy will be done, on earth as it is in heaven."

This is just one example of how He helps us harness the potential He put in families and using it for good. What a picture of how Jesus helps us overcome in this world.

Because of His willingness to submit to His creation and die and then rise up from the dead, He has given us the victory over all the evil that binds us. Hallelujah!

> But thanks be to God, who gives us the victory through our Lord Jesus Christ.
> 1 Corinthians 15:57

Glorious Mothering

Chapter 12

Finding Time for Recharge

I've spent a lot of time in this book speaking to you about how you should ratchet *up* your game. Now I am going to share how to ratchet *down*.

I know I am not alone in the feeling there are not enough hours in the day. Some days it seems as if every mili-second is taken up with something or someone important (even bathroom breaks are "on the clock" when you're a mom).

Then, when a big change comes along, it's enough to send me off to Panic-topia! I don't have the emotional reserves to deal with yet another complication. This is not good. None of us can live in a constant state of fight or flight. Everyone, and that includes moms of many, needs some of what is called "margin."

This is when the lines are slack and we can relax and float, letting all the tension dissipate.

There is a key to this whole idea, and it has nothing to do with taking a bubble bath, going to the spa, or hiring a sitter and getting away for a weekend.

Hope for the Harried

Here is an illustration of what I am talking about. Just the other night the family decided to rent one of those new action-packed hero movies. You know the type, the ones with loads of CGI and sound effects that shake the entire house.

As usual, my life had been busy, busy, busy that day and I was so tired my eyes were burning. Instead of forcing myself to sit through a ho-hum movie that I would forget seconds after it was over, I decided to do something that would be meaningful to me and my whole family; I took a nap. I took it right there on the couch while the movie was going on as loud as ever. Two hours later I awoke refreshed and ready to tackle dinner.

How was this possible? There is only one explanation; I have learned how to: IGNORE.

Instead of being drug along behind the bullet train of life, I can ignore bickering, piles of laundry, bills, dirty dishes, social media, and pleas for attention from outside sources. This gives me the space I need to:

- Clear all of the other stressers out of my mind so I can plan (instead of having my mind space taken up by a mass of confusing thoughts).

- Keep me focused so I can listen intently to a teen who is struggling with her emotions (instead of missing the entire conversation due to all the other noise in the house that demands my attention).

- Go on a walk and actually look at the sky and the clouds and bless God for His creation (instead of staring at the sidewalk and running through my list of cares and concerns).

- Cuddle next to my dear husband and adore him for the man he is (instead of thinking about all the other people that demand my love and care).

I Put Ignoring to Use By:

Purposeful Planning

After the birth of my third child in three short years, a very wise woman told me that a daily nap was not optional, it was required. Of course I thought she was a bit touched; how could I find a time for a daily nap with three children under three?

But I did. By adjusting and training I got all of those little ones to take a nap at the same time each afternoon, and in the quiet of at least a half hour each day I was able to recover and rest. In order to make this happen I forced myself to ignore the pile of laundry that needed to be put away, or those dishes I didn't quite get to, or that letter I could be writing without interruptions.

This practice continued for over 30 years. It was so ingrained in my children that I didn't have to say a word,; the house automatically became quiet for at least an hour every afternoon.

Taking Advantage of Bits and Pieces of Time Such As:

Vacuuming. Funny, but when that little motor is humming I can't hear (nor am I expected to hear) all of the little bickers, or the phone, or the call to help find a missing shoe from the other side of the house. This is an amazing way to find "mind space." While it looks like I am productively cleaning and can't be interrupted, I am actually thinking and praying. Some of the best ideas have come to me (including ones for blogging and vlogging) while I was cleaning the floor!

Waiting in the car. Even though they may be time-wasters, errands and sitting in the car are things we cannot avoid. Why not turn them into "refresh" time?

When I am in the car the world seems to stand still. There are no loads of laundry to fold, no dishes to wash, no dinner to make, no squabbles to figure out. I can grab my planner and look over my scripture meditations, my prayer list, or a psalm of praise to God.

Or, I can just close my eyes and breathe deeply while listening to some rejuvenating worship music (right now it's all Rivers and Robots).

The Bible Tells Me So

There are a number of scriptures I rely on that have helped me develop this useful skill.

The first is found in 1 Peter 5:7:

Glorious Mothering

> casting all your cares [all your anxieties, all your
> worries, and all your concerns, once and for all] on
> Him, for He cares about you [with deepest affection,
> and watches over you very carefully]. (Amplified)

Another passage which has allowed me sweet rest is
found in Psalm 127:

> {A Song of degrees for Solomon.}
> Except the LORD build the house, they labour in
> vain that build it: except the LORD keep the city, the
> watchman waketh but in vain.
> It is vain for you to rise up early, to sit up late, to eat
> the bread of sorrows: for so he giveth his beloved
> sleep.
> Lo, children are an heritage of the LORD: and the
> fruit of the womb is his reward.
> As arrows are in the hand of a mighty man; so are
> children of the youth.
> Happy is the man that hath his quiver full of them:
> they shall not be ashamed, but they shall speak with
> the enemies in the gate.

I have meditated on it for so many years that I
memorized it without trying! It seems every year God
opens another part of it to me.

The most recent revelation is verse 3 that says,
"Behold, children are an heritage of the LORD."

I had always taken that to read that children are a blessing from God. Now I realize there is another meaning, one that has set me free from a lot of potential concern.

Not only are children a blessing (heritage) *from* the Lord, they are a blessing *of* the Lord. We cooperate and allow Him to bring people into this world so they can be His heritage for His honor and His glory, and so they are also ultimately *His* responsibility. What freedom! Hallelujah!

This goes along nicely with the previous verses. While the builder and the watchman must show up and do their part, it is God who builds and watches. Solomon, the wisest man to ever live, tells us it is vain to exhaust ourselves trying to keep it all together and make it happen in our own strength.

I love what Charles Spurgeon wrote about this passage in his *Treasury of David* commentaries on the book of Psalms:

> Because the Lord is mainly to be rested in, all carking care is mere vanity and vexation of spirit. We are bound to be diligent, for this the Lord blesses; we ought not to be anxious, for that dishonours the Lord, and can never secure his favour...Of course the true believer will never be lazy or extravagant; if he should be he will have to suffer for it; but he will not think it needful or right to be worried and miserly. Faith brings calm with it, and banishes the disturbers

who both by day and by night murder peace... Through faith the Lord makes his chosen ones to rest in him in happy freedom from care...those whom the Lord loves are delivered from the fret and fume of life, and take a sweet repose upon the bosom of their Lord. He rests them; blesses them while resting; blesses them more in resting than others in their moiling and toiling. God is sure to give the best thing to his beloved, and we here see that he gives them sleep -- that is a laying aside of care, a forgetfulness of need, a quiet leaving of matters with God:

Did you catch that?

He rests them; blesses them while resting; blesses them more in resting than others in their moiling and toiling.

As if these were not enough, here are a few more passages that solidify the whole idea:

And He said to me, "My grace is sufficient for you, for My strength is made perfect in weakness." Therefore most gladly I will rather boast in my infirmities, that the power of Christ may rest upon me. Therefore I take pleasure in infirmities, in reproaches, in needs, in persecutions, in distresses, for Christ's sake. For when I am weak, then I am strong.
2 Corinthians 12:9-10

Of course, I do my part. Every day I show up and

put all of what I have written in this book into practical application.

But then, after I have done everything I'm supposed to do, I can rest, knowing He will take my efforts and multiply them by His amazing power and grace.

Chapter 13

Troubleshooting

So far, we've been going over one theory after another, with a few concrete examples and a smidgen of practical application mixed in for good measure.

While that is all fine and dandy, there is more to the story—*your* story, that is.

There are things in our lives we will not be able to change, such as our lineage or the color of our eyes. There are some circumstances that we won't be able to alter, such as the state of the economy, a debilitating illness, or the thoughtless acts and intentions of another human being.

For these we accept, adapt, and pray.

But there are other things we absolutely should strive to change. If we don't we will reap the consequences, be they large or small. This is our moral obligation and duty as Christian women; a way we can show our gratitude and love to God.

So, besides offering theory, I want to leave you with actual practical ways you can wrestle the hindrances in your life and come out victorious!

First, Sit and Think of the Places Where There is No Rest

Count back to the beginning of each day or week and recall what causes your brows to furrow or your chest to tighten. Then, sit down and make out a list of the pressure spots.

Examples:

- Meal times are frantic.

- The bathrooms are always a mess.

- We can never find matching socks.

- The kids' bedrooms are always a mess.

- It takes forever to get the kids into bed.

- Toothbrushes are always lost.

- The car is always trashed.

- I can never get out of my sweats!

- I can't find any time to spend with the Lord.

- The house is always upside-down when Daddy gets home.

- There is never a moment's peace when Daddy gets home.

- There is never a moment's peace when *I* am home!

Glorious Mothering

- The kids are constantly losing their homeschool books and supplies.

- I can't keep track of all of these kids' homeschooling.

- The little ones are always sabotaging our learning time.

- I can't seem to get anyone's cooperation.

- No one comes when I call.

- The kids' clothes are never matched and usually wrinkled and unwearable unless I iron them.

- Going out of the house is always so exhausting.

- We can't keep the floors clean.

- I have an adequate amount of money for food, but it doesn't seem to stretch.

- The laundry is out of hand.

- I don't know if I'm prepared to receive our new baby.

- I can never find a pen when I need one.

- I'm not getting enough sleep.

- I can't find time to take care of my appearance.

Second, Pray

Dear Father,

I am so glad that You care for even the smallest parts of my life. I confess that I have been carrying worries and stresses that have been stealing my peace. I cast them all on You Lord, because I know You care for me, and I ask that You grant me wisdom to tackle each area, believing in faith that you have answers for me and thanking You for them in advance.

In the precious, powerful name of Jesus, Amen.

Third, Honestly Observe and Then Assess the Situation Using These Questions:

- Is the problem a matter of lack of proper tools and supplies?

- Is there a lack of organization of tools and supplies that I *do* have?

- Is the problem too much stuff?

- Is the flow inefficient?

- Is there a lack of well-defined boundaries?

- Is there too much time allotted?

- Is there a need for a precisely spelled-out procedure that can be followed easily?

- Is the present procedure too hard or too complicated?

- Is there a lack of follow-through on my part?

Fourth, research the problem.

There are many sources for this:

- A good book

- A friend or relative

- A blog post or two

- A YouTube or other type of video

This doesn't always produce a solution, and can actually sometimes add more stress if one is not careful. But quite often God helps me to discover at least a direction in which to go when I begin to search for answers.

Fifth, Take a mental Trip With Your Imagination Concerning the Problem

For instance, if there is an issue with after dinner clean up, take the time to go over precisely how you are currently operating. Pin-point the actual stressers:

- The dishes are being left on the table.

- It takes an hour for the dishes to be washed and/or put into the dishwasher.

- The floors are a mess during the operation.

- The food is not being properly put away in the refrigerator.

- The children spend a lot of time bickering while cleaning.

- The clean dishes are not being put away properly .

- The stove top and counters are not being cleaned properly.

- The trash overflows onto the floor while the children are cleaning.

- No one seems to know what his/her job really is.

Sixth, Brainstorm Some Possible Solutions

"Brainstorming" means that you are throwing anything and everything onto the canvas, whether it looks like it will actually work or not.

Mind-mapping on a huge sheet of paper can help, but most of the time I use a number of index cards with the name of one problem printed at the top of each.

After you are finished emptying your mind of any and all ideas, then start eliminating the absolutely silly ones and look more closely at the ones you think just might work.

Then, Sleep On It

I will praise the LORD, who counsels me;

Glorious Mothering

Even at night my heart instructs me."
Psalm 16:7 NIV

This is to problem solving as time in the oven is to cake making. It is not enough to have all of the information and possible solutions; you have to let them stir and ruminate until a picture forms in your mind.

Many, many times I will awaken in the morning knowing exactly what I should do...

Communicate With Your Family and Make a Plan

After you have a clear direction, start putting a plan in place and then a way to communicate it so that it will be made clear to everyone.

Along with not being especially energetic, I am also not keen on wasting time talking about a problem. My natural urge is just to dig in and get 'er done. However, it only took a few flopped attempts to realize that I must never, ever skip the crucial step of communicating with my "team," no matter if it takes an hour or so. Over the years I have come up with numerous ways to get my points across.

My first move is to call everyone to a meeting and explain the situation.

Sometimes I need to be stern, but there is always room for a bit of humor as well. Little kids, especially, love exaggeration, so I try and build pictures in their minds of dirty underwear stretching to the moon, or a man who couldn't find his toothbrush so his teeth became so dirty they grew hair.

I know I have their attention and imagination as soon as I have them all laughing. I also ask them questions, such as, "Whoever is tired of so much yelling in the morning, raise your hand," etc. Then I lead them down the lane of logic; I give them reasons why things need to improve, and then I offer up some solutions. I might even tell them I am open to any of their positive, helpful suggestions (the little ones can sometimes surprise us with amazing clarity and ingenuity--and oftentimes they get us giggling with their sweet attempts to "help").

By this time, they are usually pretty emotionally invested (they feel a sense of ownership), so it's not hard at all to get them motivated to follow a new scheme. This is when the magic begins. It is one thing to have a mom who is energized, but when a whole house full of children gets energized, watch out!

Chapter 14

Don't Make Your Kids Ashamed of Their Home

A while back a carpenter came in to measure our kitchen cabinets for replacement. He was immediately shocked to find how good they looked. It seems he had been in numerous houses in our area whose cabinets did not fare as well. Other homes built at the same time were missing doors, drawers, etc. This was more remarkable to him when he learned how many people we have in our family.

This was possible because we had maintained these cupboards over the years. Whenever we encountered a problem we promptly took screw-gun in hand and fixed it. We also routinely scrubbed and oiled the cabinet faces so that they would look as presentable as possible.

There are some large families who think we are silly. They refuse to fix or take care of anything because they expect that their kids will just ruin their good efforts anyway. So they live in tumble-down conditions with ripped screens and torn couches.

What they don't realize is they and their children are missing out on many of the blessings of keeping up on things, and their actions and attitudes speak loudly that they do not consider their children worthy of nice surroundings.

Teach Them Respect

Yes, kids can be hard on things; They don't shut cupboards and drawers gently, they sit down heavily on couches, and they jump on beds. How does a dad and mom cope with a house full of monkeys?

One of the first, and easiest, things we have done is to train our children to be more respectful of their surroundings. This one takes diligent attention, and none of us is 100% successful, but we can definitely make dents in normal childish tendencies. Here are a few ways to go about it:

- For banging a door shut, children can practice closing it properly five times.

- For disrespecting the furniture (jumping, scratching, writing on), they may lose the privilege of sitting on it or using it for one or more days.

- Make them scrub and paint to remove the marks off of the walls and floors.

- Check daily for fingerprints on door jambs and light

fixtures and make them responsible for keeping these surfaces clean.

- When they are outrageously neglectful or destructive, make them pay to repair/replace the things they damage out of their own pockets, or at least with their own sweat-equity.

- Take them to the model homes builders fix up as showcases and let them see first-hand how nice a house can be.

- Teach them that treating things properly means they last longer and are nicer for your own family.

Maintain What You Have

This is a big one with my dear husband, who loves to keep his cars and anything he owns as good or better than the day he bought them. (He often reminds them to "take care of your things and they will take care of you.").

This means that we tighten screws, wash and paint walls, shampoo carpets, and sew up rips. It's not just Mom and Dad that are involved, but everyone learns how. This is good for children; it saves money and teaches them important skills that will bless them as adults.

Fill Your Home With Nice Things

Next, as you are laying the foundation of respectful behavior and maintaining as a family values, be sure and fill your home with nice things.

Now, this doesn't necessarily mean new and expensive. It just means that you use the money, time, and energy you have to its best benefit in creating an atmosphere that says to your children,

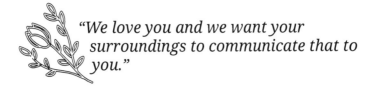

"We love you and we want your surroundings to communicate that to you."

My husband and I have had so much fun doing this over the years. We have made it a habit to start shopping for household needs long before we have the money. This allows us to educate ourselves on what is the best for our bucks.

For example, when looking for something like a set of dresser drawers we have found it may be better to purchase older furniture that has been made better than to purchase the cheapest new furniture because it is convenient and "in style". We can always make it nicer by fixing, polishing, or painting it as necessary.

There are also times when older or cheaper is definitely *not* better. We purchased a number of second-hand, cloth-covered couch sets that we thought were cheaper before we realized that dishing out the extra cash for quality leather couches was more frugal in the long-run.

On the other hand, for some high-wear items it may be better to purchase the cheapest and replace it often.

Glorious Mothering

There are simply some things that are going to break, no matter how hard we try and keep them up. It is next to impossible to find something made well enough in today's world that will last indefinitely.

Take dishes, for instance. It doesn't matter how we monitor things, children and young people sometimes have trouble handling heavy plates, cups, etc. that are slippery from the dishwater. I decided long ago that I could either wring my hands and blow my top, or I could adapt. Therefore, I purchase my dishes as cheaply as possible; either from a discount store or from the Goodwill. Very rarely do they match (even though we currently only buy white onces).

Then, when a 29 cent bowl breaks (I look for the ones that are discounted), I am totally relaxed Besides, it's fun to take some pocket changes go and pick out new dishes, and makes for an interesting table, too!

It's Worth the Trouble

I'm not suggesting that any of this is easy, or that there aren't times when making extra efforts doesn't drain you. Some days it seems as though I have trouble keeping up with it all and I am tempted to give up and give in.

That's when I stop, look, and listen. My people *like* to be here. They feel blessed and comfortable knowing that things are in order. *They are not ashamed to invite their friends to visit.*

(My daughter wanted me to make sure and insert

that kids can help you relax by contributing on their own initiative. She says love is give-and-take and most children like the idea that cleaning up by themselves helps Mom out.)

Somewhere in our house someone is praying or reading the Word. Somewhere a tiny child is being consoled by an older sibling or someone is giggling. And somewhere out there are growing families that had their spiritual foundations built here; godly couples raising precious children for his purposes.

No matter where I might live, I would be battling, but God blessed me and gave me the desires of my heart so that I would have the privilege of defending *this* home, and *these* people.

You Are the Queen of Your Home

If things are not going well, there is nowhere else to look for blame but in the mirror. Yes, this means great responsibility, but it also means great power. How will you wield it? If you are up to the challenge, you will fall down in prayer, rise up to battle, and then conquer in the name of the Lord!

Glorious Mothering

Homeschool Products
by Sherry K. Hayes
Available on Amazon.com

make ALL of your learning count

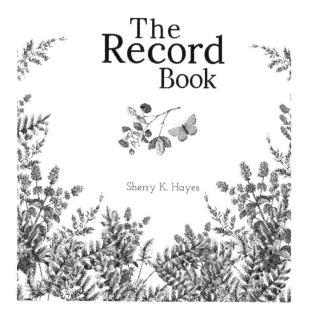

The
Record
Book

Sherry K. Hayes

The Record Book

Learning is more than textbooks and tests. It is a living, active thing, and it is happening all of the time. The problem is capturing it and recording it so that it counts. The Record Book makes that seem simple! With these pages you will:

• Have a record for authorities

• Be able to accurately produce high school transcripts

• Have a bank of memories both for sentimental and practical use later on.

Each page includes places to write down the activity, the time spent, the children who were involved, and the education area(s) covered. There is also a place for notes, such as the attitude of the children, the circumstances of the day, or even some directions for the next day.

level three

THE
LESSON
BOOK

*The
Lesson
Books*

level one

THE
LESSON
BOOK

level two

THE
LESSON
BOOK

level four

THE
LESSON
BOOK

level five

THE
LESSON
BOOK

The Lesson Book is meant to be something that brings peace and rest to moms while giving children more freedom and enjoyment in learning. This is not a workbook. Workbooks ask specific questions and require specific answers. This one is not about specifics, just about giving a framework so that you, the teacher, have less work to do. YOU decide what needs to be copied and dictated. Your child decides what is important enough to be recorded. Besides the written word, there are plenty of spaces for drawings and doodlings (or anything else you want to add, such as a clipping of a picture or a bunch of stickers).

The Lesson Book: Level One
This one is for those children who are beginning to understand the basics of word composition and are sounding out simple sentences.

The Lesson Book: Level Two
This one is for those children who are doing well at reading whole sentences and paragraphs and have a good understanding as to the construction of words and sentences.

The Lesson Book: Level Three
This one is for those children who are becoming more comfortable with reading and writing so they no longer need guidelines as in primary lessons.

The Lesson Book: Level Four
This one is for those children who are fluent readers but are building on their vocabulary and writing skills.

The Lesson Book: Level Five
This one is for those children who are confident readers and writers but need to be challenged in fluidity, complexity, and higher vocabulary.

Gentle Grammar

Level Four

· gentle · GRAMMAR

An Adaptation of New Language Exercises for Primary Schools
by C. C. Long

Level Three

· gentle · GRAMMAR

An Adaptation of New Language Exercises for Primary Schools
by C. C. Long

Level One

· gentle · GRAMMAR

An Adaptation of New Language Exercises for Primary Schools
by C. C. Long

Level Two

· gentle · GRAMMAR

An Adaptation of New Language Exercises for Primary Schools
by C. C. Long

This program is:

- Something you can put on "auto pilot"—little to no preparation or input on your part
- Quick (for kids who already have trouble sitting still for reading and math)
- Not technical
- Inexpensive

With these little books your faltering readers will quickly turn into competent, confident writers of sentences and paragraphs, something that is essential for those of us who enjoy to homeschool with notebooking.

Gentle Grammar: Level 1
This level is for children who are reading whole words and sentences pretty well. If your child can read an en-tire Dr. Seuss book pretty easily, he's probably ready.

Gentle Grammar: Level 2
You won't want your child to attempt this level until he/she has a good understanding of the different types of sentences and has a basic grasp of punctuation. If he is not used to these things, have him go through the first level of Gentle Grammar before you try this second level.

Gentle Grammar: Level 3
You won't want your child to attempt this level until he/she has a good understanding of the different types of sentences and has a basic grasp of punctuation. If he is not used to these things, have him go through the first and second levels of Gentle Grammar before you try this third level.

Gentle Grammar: Level 4
You won't want your child to attempt this level until he/she has a good understanding of the different types of sentences and has a basic grasp of punctuation. The best preparation for this fourth level is the first, second and third levels of Gentle Grammar.

Printed in Great Britain
by Amazon

34694898R00085